Waiting For Yesterday

A Play

Duncan Greenwood

Samuel French – London
New York – Sydney – Toronto – Hollywood

FOR AMATEUR PRODUCTION ENQUIRIES

UNITED KINGDOM AND WORLD
EXCLUDING NORTH AMERICA
plays@samuelfrench.co.uk
020 7255 4302/01

Each title is subject to availability from Samuel French,
depending upon country of performance.

CHARACTERS

Mrs Dalmahoy
Alex Dalmahoy, her daughter
Don Peters
Mrs McEwan
Miss Fanner
Lt. Colonel Blanchard
Mrs Roski
Mrs O'Neil

The action of the play takes place in the lounge of a private hotel in Bayswater

Time—the present

Character descriptions

Mrs Dalmahoy: Elderly. A hard domineering woman. Used to getting her own way.

Alex Dalmahoy: Her daughter. In her middle thirties. Quiet, sensitive and intelligent but plain and not exceptionally attractive in appearance.

Don Peters: In his late thirties. Smart and cynical. Ruthless and determined to achieve his own ends.

Mrs McEwan: An elderly Scotswoman. Pleasant, good-natured and understanding.

Miss Fanner: An elderly spinster. Quiet, timid and sensitive with a rather simple and sentimental outlook on life.

Lt. Colonel Blanchard: Elderly retired regular army officer. Generous and good-natured. In no way resembles the traditional Colonel Blimp.

Mrs Roski: Elderly expatriate Pole. Level-headed and philosophical. Speaks with an accent.

Mrs O'Neil: An elderly Irishwoman. Warm-hearted, quick-tempered with a great sense of fun. Speaks with an Irish intonation.

To John Chilvers

Photo: Nor Davies, Swansea

ACT I*

The lounge of a private hotel in Bayswater. A Friday evening in spring

The hotel was once a Georgian residence and the room is therefore spacious with a high ceiling. It is tastelessly decorated and has the air of threadbare gentility. R is an upright piano below which, on a small occasional table, is an old but still functional radio set. In the back wall R french windows lead to a small garden. It is completely enclosed by high brick walls which are the backs of adjoining properties. To the L of the french windows is a door giving access to the rest of the hotel. DL is a large ornate fireplace in the hearth of which stands a slow combustion stove. Above the fireplace is an easy chair. A settee is set obliquely facing the fireplace. Below the fireplace is a writing desk. There are a number of other easy chairs in the room, all covered in faded chintz loose covers

When the CURTAIN rises, Mrs Dalmahoy is sitting at the piano playing. Alex, her daughter, is standing L of the piano, singing. The song is one of Amy Woodford Finden's Indian Love Lyrics

Alex (*singing*) "Pale hands I love . . ."
Mrs Dalmahoy (*stopping playing*) No Alex. No. No. No. It's "love"—(*she strikes the correct note*)—not "love". (*She strikes a note a semi-tone lower*) Try again.
Alex (*singing*) "Pale hands I love——"

She hits the right note. Mrs Dalmahoy nods approval

"—beside the Shalimar . . ."
Mrs Dalmahoy (*repeating the last four chords*) "Shalimar-ha". (*Repeating the last two chords*) "Mar-ha".
Alex (*singing*) "Pale hand I love beside the Shalimar-ha. Where are you now? Who lies beneath your spell——
Mrs Dalmahoy (*hitting a discord in exasperation*) No! No! No!

Alex throws the sheet of music she is holding on to the top of the piano and, almost in tears, marches to the door

Alex!

---

*N.B. Paragraph 3 on page ii of this Acting Edition regarding photocopying and video-recording should be carefully read.

Alex pauses for a moment and then sweeps out of the door almost colliding with Don Peters, who enters as she leaves. Alex gives a short "Sorry" as she goes. Don, who is carrying a book, looks curiously after her and then turns to Mrs Dalmahoy

Don Good-evening.

Mrs Dalmahoy Good-evening. I hope you'll excuse my daughter.

Don For what?

Mrs Dalmahoy Her show of temperament.

Don I didn't notice.

Mrs Dalmohoy She's so stubborn. Three days she's got. That's all. Three days to her audition and she behaves like this. I hope it hasn't disturbed you.

Don Disturbed me?

Mrs Dalmahoy Her practising. We try to keep to times which will cause least annoyance to the other residents. Six-thirty to seven in the evening when everyone's at dinner.

Don And seven-thirty to eight in the morning when everyone's getting up.

Mrs Dalmahoy You can hear from your room?

Don Quite distinctly. Since my arrival three days ago I haven't found it necessary to set the alarm.

Mrs Dalmahoy I'm sorry.

Don There's no need to apologize. I find shaving to the strains of "Kingfisher Blue-hoo-hoo" a stimulating experience.

Mrs Dalmahoy Really?

Don Yes. It helps my morning defecation no end.

Mrs Dalmahoy So you don't like Amy Woodford Finden.

Don Functionally yes. Musically no.

Mrs Dalmahoy (*sarcastically*) I presume your taste in music is more contemporary.

Don My taste is catholic. I enjoy the work of a wide range of composers from Mozart onwards. But there are gaps. Amy Woodford Finden is one of them.

Mrs Dalmahoy (*changing the subject*) Are you staying here long?

Don I don't know. Are you?

Mrs Dalmahoy My daughter and I spend three months here every year. In the spring of course. In the summer we go to the country and we winter in France.

Don Most impressive.

Mrs Dalmahoy It has been our custom ever since my husband died. But things are not the same here as they used to be. The place gets shabbier, the staff become more indifferent and the permanent residents get older. But returning has become a habit which we find difficult to break. (*She gathers up her music*) I must find my daughter. She's probably locked herself in her bedroom. And that means practising is over for this evening. In any case the other residents will be coming in from dinner soon. Have you tried the dinner?

Don The first night.

Mrs Dalmahoy And since?

Don Bernotti's. Down the road.

Mrs Dalmahoy Very wise. We don't dine here in the evening either. If we did we wouldn't get a chance to use the piano. Not that the lounge is extensively used in the evenings. Most of them go to their own rooms. It's mainly the ones that can't afford ten p for the gas fire that come in here. (*She looks at her watch*) It's almost time for Miss Fanner. She's generally the first. She skips the dessert to make sure of getting the chair nearest the fireplace. I expect you've met her.

Don No. I've been out every evening since I arrived.

Mrs Dalmahoy Then you can expect a good attendance if you remain in tonight. Your presence might even attract some of the hermits. They only come in here when someone new arrives.

Don Out of curiosity?

Mrs Dalmahoy Partly. Their main object is to find a new audience to listen to their dreary little life stories. It's quite an event for them Mr ... er ... Peters, isn't it?

Don That's right.

Mrs Dalmahoy I thought it must be. Though the visitors' book isn't much help. You haven't signed it yet.

Don Then Mrs McEwan must have told you my name.

Mrs Dalmahoy She didn't as a matter of fact. There was a letter addressed to you in the rack this morning.

Don You're very observant.

Mrs Dalmahoy No, Mr Peters, just curious. I must go.

Mrs McEwan enters

Mrs McEwan Oh. Good-evening.

Mrs Dalmahoy }
Don } (*together*) Good-evening.

Mrs Dalmahoy I've just been telling your new guest that he's breaking the law.

Mrs McEwan and Don exchange glances

Mrs McEwan Really?

Mrs Dalmahoy He hasn't signed the visitors' book yet.

Mrs McEwan Oh. It's on the desk over there, Mr Peters.

Don I'll sign it now. (*He crosses to the desk and signs the book*)

Mrs Dalmahoy Your normal punctilliousness over signing the book does not appear to apply to Mr Peters, Mrs McEwan.

Mrs McEwan It was an oversight on my part.

Mrs Dalmahoy Of course. Good-night.

She gives a disbelieving smile and exits

Mrs McEwan I hope you're finding everything satisfactory.

Don On the whole. Except the dinner.

Mrs McEwan I would of course like to put on a more varied menu. But apart from the staffing problem ...

Don There are the catering costs.

Mrs McEwan Exactly. I can't match the Savoy Grill for forty pounds a week all in.

Don You could get a bit nearer if you charged more.

Mrs McEwan There's no point in it now.

Don But you could have done it before. You haven't increased your terms for at least four years.

Mrs McEwan I know. But then you see most of them are on fixed incomes. They wouldn't have been able to pay.

Don Too bad.

Mrs McEwan I couldn't have faced turning them out. They'd have had nowhere to go.

Don That'd have been their problem. You'd have filled the vacancies with no trouble.

Mrs McEwan It isn't as easy as all that, Mr Peters. I've known them all well. For years.

Don You can't run a business on sentiment, Mrs McEwan.

Mrs McEwan That's one way of looking at it.

Don It's the only way if you want to succeed.

Mrs McEwan I've done quite well.

Don But not well enough. I wouldn't be here if you had.

Mrs McEwan It's not going to be easy to tell them.

Don I'm sure it isn't.

Mrs McEwan You could help me there.

Don Sorry. That isn't my job.

Miss Fanner enters

Miss Fanner Good-evening. (*She smiles and nods to Mrs McEwan and then turns to Don expecting to be introduced*)

Don gives her a quick nod and a smile, turns away and sits on the settee

Mrs McEwan Good-evening, Miss Fanner.

Miss Fanner The singing lesson finished very abruptly this evening.

Mrs McEwan I don't think Alex was feeling up to it.

Miss Fanner What a pity. I enjoy listening to her. She has such a sweet voice. It's remarkable the progress she's made. I'm sure the audition will go well.

Mrs McEwan I'm sure it will. Excuse me.

Mrs McEwan exits

Miss Fanner sits in the chair above the fireplace. There is a slight pause whilst she wonders how to open up a conversation with Don who is now reading his book

Miss Fanner It's still very cold for this time of the year isn't it?

Don (*looking up from his book*) I hadn't really noticed. (*He carries on reading*)

There is a pause

Miss Fanner I visited the sunken garden this afternoon and there was quite a sharp wind. (*A pause*) It drove me into the Orangery. (*A pause*) I do hope we don't get any frost. The tulips will suffer and they look so lovely at the moment. (*A pause*) Do you ever go?

Don Go? Go where?

Miss Fanner To the sunken garden.

Don I've never heard of it.

Miss Fanner It's near the Round Pond in Kensington Gardens. Only a few minutes walk away.

Don Oh. (*He resumes his reading*)

Miss Fanner I go there every day. It really is delightful at this time of year. If you're staying here for a while I can thoroughly recommend a visit.

Don I'm afraid I shan't have the time.

Miss Fanner What a pity. The spring flowers really are worth seeing. They last such a little time. Further south, in the Mediterranean they'll be all over by now. Have you ever been on the Continent Mr ... er ...

Don Peters.

Miss Fanner Mr Peters?

Don Often.

Miss Fanner Really? Which parts?

Don Holland, France, Spain ...

Miss Fanner Spain? Now that's interesting. I know Spain well. I lived there for many years. Which part do you know?

Don Andalusia.

Miss Fanner But how extraordinary. I've spent over twenty years in Seville. I was governess there to a very wealthy family. Their name was Carreras. I don't know if you've come across them.

Don Andalusia's quite a sizeable province ...

Miss Fanner They're quite well known. They have large estates. Oranges mostly. But vineyards as well.

Lieutenant-Colonel Blanchard enters

Ah Colonel! Have you met Mr Peters?

Colonel Not formally. But as we occupy adjacent tables in the dining-room we have exchanged greetings. I hope you're being made comfortable.

Don The place is reasonable ... for the price.

Colonel I think it's excellent. Mrs McEwan looks after us very well. Makes us all feel at home. (*Crossing to the window*) Can't expect more than that. (*Looking out of the window*) Seen your azalea this evening Miss Fanner?

Miss Fanner I had a quick peep at it before dinner.

Colonel Did you count the blooms on it? I make it ten.

Miss Fanner And at least three more to come.

Colonel Interested in gardening, Mr Peters?

Don Not a bit.

Colonel Hm. Then you won't have noticed our modest little plot here outside the window.

Don You're right. I haven't.

Colonel It survives pretty well considering it's hemmed in by bricks and mortar.

Miss Fanner You should have seen it five years ago, Mr Peters. Rubble rubbish and willow herb. A meeting place for all the cats of the district.

Colonel It was the cats that prompted us to do something about it.

Miss Fanner No it wasn't Colonel. It was the willow herb. Don't you remember that evening when all the seeds kept blowing into the room?

Colonel You're quite right.

Miss Fanner And you said "If that rubbish dump can grow willow herb it can grow roses".

Colonel We didn't waste much time after that. You took me at my word and packed me off to Whitesides the very next day to buy a spade.

Miss Fanner Everyone lent a hand. Moving the rubble and building the rockery.

Colonel And everyone bought a plant. Even Mrs McEwan.

Miss Fanner It's some compensation when you've been used to enjoying a garden. When I was a girl we had a huge plot at Maidenhead stretching right down to the river. And the Colonel had four acres in Surrey.

Colonel Still have. Got tenants in the place now though. God knows what sort of a mess it's in. But when my wife's recovered and we go back I'll soon pull it into shape again.

Miss Fanner I only hope they'll give me my old room back when I return to Seville. It looked out on to the rose garden. Up the side of the house there was bougainvillaea and right outside the window an orange tree. In April when the blossom was out it scented the whole room.

Colonel In the meantime you'll just have to make do with Mrs Roski's night scented stock. You'd better start thinking about what individual plant you'd like to see in the garden, Mr Peters. If you stay any length of time I'll be approaching you for a contribution towards it.

Mrs O'Neil enters. She spends most of her time making rugs and carries an uncompleted one under her arm

Mrs O'Neil Evening one and all.

Colonel Good-evening Mrs O'Neil. I don't think you've met our new guest—Mr Peters.

Don Good-evening.

Mrs O'Neil I'm glad to know you. But you must excuse me for a moment. I want to look round the estate before dark. To see how me lilies are doing. Hang on to that for me Colonel.

She thrusts the rug into the Colonel's hands and goes out through the french windows

Miss Fanner Give it to me, Colonel.

He hands the rug to her

I don't think she'll mind if we take a little peep at it. (*She unrolls the rug. It is almost complete*) She's certainly getting on. Another week or so and it'll be finished.

Colonel Hm. Got more patience than me. I couldn't sit night after night tying knots in little bits of wool.

Miss Fanner (*admiring the rug*) What a lovely pattern. Quite oriental.

Colonel That's not surprising. It's for her daughter in India, isn't it?

Miss Fanner They all are. This is the fifth she's made since she came here. I hope the girl appreciates what she's doing. She never seems to write.

Colonel They're all like that these days. Take everything for granted.

Miss Fanner Nonsense, Colonel. My boys write to me regularly. I always get a little gift on my birthday. And last time Carlos was in England he took me out to dinner at the Cumberland. Twice.

Colonel Of course. He's a Spaniard. All Latins are the same. They take a pride in being gallant. It would have been a different story if you'd been governess to an English family.

Miss Fanner I don't agree. I'm sure it's because they think something of me. If I thought otherwise I'd be admitting failure.

Mrs O'Neil returns from the garden. She stares at the rug spread out upon Miss Fanner's knees

(*Realizing*) Oh! I hope you don't mind, dear. We were just admiring your rug. It's coming on very well.

Mrs O'Neil So's your azalea. Can't say the same for my lilies of the valley. They're like me. Spreading in all directions.

Colonel That's nothing to worry about.

Mrs O'Neil Don't you believe it. I can't get into that frock I only bought two months ago.

Colonel I was referring to your lilies. They're healthy enough.

Mrs O'Neil There's not a flower on them. Not even a bud. It's manure they'll be wanting, Colonel. Or maybe a drop of water.

Mrs Roski enters

Colonel Ah! Mrs Roski. You're just the person we need. Mrs O'Neil's lilies need watering. Can you help?

Mrs Roski She vill have to wait. I am not allowed to put the 'ose-pipe through my bedroom vindow until it is dark. Mrs McEwan forbids it. She 'as no licence from the Vater Men to use a hose-pipe.

Colonel Oh, come now. Rules are made to be broken.

Mrs Roski Not where I come from. (*She turns to Don*) Who is our new guest?

Colonel Oh, I'm sorry. This is Mrs Roski—Mr Peters.

Don Good-evening.

Mrs Roski Good-evening. Ve 'ave seen each other in the dining-room at breakfast. But not at dinner. You do not take dinner?

Don Not here.

Mrs Roski Ah! You are a man who respects his stomach. I vish I could afford to do the same.

Miss Fanner Oh, come Mrs Roski, the meals here are quite good.

Mrs Roski They are terrible.

Mrs O'Neil It's the kitchen staff. They don't bother.

Mrs Roski And vy do they not bother? Because they are not supervized. (*To Miss Fanner*) And that is your fault.

Miss Fanner (*in surprise*) My fault?

Mrs Roski For your behaviour this evening.

Miss Fanner (*perplexed*) My behaviour?

Mrs Roski At dinner. You left your salad because it vas unvashed.

Miss Fanner Surely you didn't expect me to eat it!

Mrs Roski No. I expected you to complain.

Miss Fanner I never make scenes, Mrs Roski.

Mrs Roski Then you must expect your salad always to remain unvashed.

Miss Fanner If Mrs McEwan sees I have not touched my salad then she will do something about it.

Mrs Roski That is what you hope.

Miss Fanner Of course.

Mrs Roski It is not enough. You must do more than just hope. You must do something positive to assist the fulfillment of that hope.

Colonel And what positive action are you taking Mrs Roski to fulfil your hope of returning to Poland?

Mrs Roski It is not in my power to change the regime in my country. But it is in Miss Fanner's power to complain about her dirty lettuce. In any case, returning to Poland is not a priority. Finding my son again is all that I hope for.

There is a short silence. They have all heard this before

You all think I am crazy, eh?

Colonel Of course we don't.

Mrs Roski A foolish old woman chasing rainbows ...

Colonel Not at all. But ... well ... it's so long ago now ...

Mrs Roski Time does not matter. He is alive. I am convinced. A grown man. Living in America.

Colonel You've got the proof? At last?

Mrs Roski (*shrugging*) Proof vill only come when I see him again. But now I 'ave great 'ope. A refugee organization 'ave just written to me from America. They have traced a family called Kubanek.

Colonel Kubanek?

Mrs Roski My neighbours. Who cared for him after the air raid. When I was in hospital.

Colonel But you can't be sure it's them.

Mrs Roski One can never be sure. But one can hope. And then do something positive about it. I am saving to go to America in the autumn to find out.

Miss Fanner But this is wonderful news, Mrs Roski. I'm so glad for you. The autumn will certainly see a thinning out in our ranks. It's October when your daughter comes back from India for good, isn't it Mrs O'Neil?

Mrs O'Neil That's what she tells me. But she won't want me living with her. She has got a husband.

Miss Fanner So you'll not be leaving us after all?

Mrs O'Neil I might. It'll depend on where they settle down. If it's a long way from London maybe I'll buy a cottage somewhere near them. So I can baby-sit for my grandchildren—if and when they arrive. And me daughter can pop in and cry on me shoulder from time to time when her husband beats her too hard.

Miss Fanner Surely he wouldn't do that!

Mrs O'Neil Why not? Mine did, God rest his soul.

Colonel Well at least I'll still be here in the autumn. Unless of course my wife gets better.

Miss Fanner I certainly won't. I'll be back in Seville.

Colonel It's definite then?

Miss Fanner Yes, I got a letter from Carlos two weeks ago. His wife's expecting the baby in August.

Mrs O'Neil But you told me you were going out as governess not as nursemaid.

Miss Fanner I like to be there at the beginning.

Colonel So you'll go out in August?

Miss Fanner They haven't specified a date yet. But they will. I went back when Carlos was only two weeks old. It was different with his father, Roddy.

Mrs O'Neil Roddy?

Miss Fanner That's what I called him. Rodriques Alonzo Don Miguel was far too much of a mouthful for me. He was my first baby. And four years old when I took up the appointment. It only seems yesterday. And now he's going to be a grandfather.

Mrs O'Neil I must say I hand it to you, Miss Fanner. Teaching the three Rs to three consecutive generations. But then you've been lucky.

Miss Fanner Lucky?

Mrs O'Neil Working for Spaniards. They breed like flies. With any other nationality you'd never have covered more than two.

Miss Fanner I'm not counting my chickens yet, Mrs O'Neil. The third generation isn't here yet.

Mrs O'Neil Don't be so pessimistic. The bun's cooking in the oven. No-one's likely to turn out the gas.

Mrs Dalmahoy enters, carrying her music. Alex follows her

Mrs Dalmahoy I have a message from Mrs McEwan. She's asked me to remind you all that Mr Slack will be on BBC Television in five minutes time. If anyone wants to see him in colour they are welcome to go to her private sitting-room.

Miss Fanner That's very kind of her. Her room's much cosier than the television room. I'd like to see him for one. How about you, Colonel?

Colonel The last time we saw him he wasn't very good.

Mrs Roski I did not recognize him in all those whiskers.

Colonel I suppose we ought to make the effort. He mentioned it to me the other day.

Miss Fanner Me too. He'll be hurt if he thinks no-one's shown any interest. How about you, Mr Peters?

Don (*looking up from his book*) Me?

Miss Fanner Would you like to see Mr Slack in a play on television?

Don Who's Mr Slack?

Miss Fanner He's a resident here.

Colonel Sits at the table behind you in the dining-room.

Don The little man with the bald head and glasses?

Mrs O'Neil That's right. He looks like a bank clerk. But he's really an actor. He specializes in grocer's parts on ITV commercials.

Miss Fanner That's hardly fair. I've seen him in a lot of detergent commercials.

Mrs O'Neil And with that well-scrubbed appearance he's got they suit him better too. Still, scrubbed or otherwise I don't imagine you'll be interested in watching his performance, Mr Peters?

Don No, not really.

Mrs O'Neil Neither am I. But I'm going because the poor fellow'll only quiz me about it tomorrow. I can still get on with me rug when he isn't on. (*She picks up her rug and moves to the door*) You'd better come as well, Mrs Roski. I want more wool cutting.

Mrs Roski (*rising and moving to the door with a sigh*) Clip, clip, clip! All I do is clip her wool for her!

Mrs O'Neil exits followed by Mrs Roski

Colonel (*moving to the door*) The last time we went into Mrs McEwan's room to see television she gave us all a drink.

Miss Fanner It was Christmas Eve. (*She follows him to the door*)

Colonel (*disappointed*) So it was. Not a hope I suppose at this time of the year?

Miss Fanner I don't think so. Unless it happens to be your birthday.

Colonel My birthday? (*He pauses and smiles*) Yes, why not? After you, Miss Fanner.

Miss Fanner exits, followed by the Colonel

Mrs Dalmahoy (*hovering near the piano*) Have you had dinner yet, Mr Peters?

Don (*looking up from his book*) Dinner? No. I eat later.

Mrs Dalmahoy How long do Bernotti's remain open?

Don Until midnight. Why? Are you thinking of joining me?

Mrs Dalmahoy Good gracious me, no. We have our own favourite restaurant. A little further up the road.

Don You want to get rid of me? Is that it?

Mrs Dalmahoy Certainly not. It's just that . . .

Don Don't apologize. If you want to continue practising again I'll go to my room. I can read just as well there. (*He rises*)

Mrs Dalmahoy That's very kind of you . . .

Alex (*sitting down on the settee*) Don't go, Mr Peters. There'll be no more practising this evening as far as I'm concerned.

Mrs Dalmahoy Alex! You said upstairs . . .

Alex I said I'd consider it if there was no-one in the lounge.

Don (*making a move towards the door*) I'll leave you to it.

Alex No please! Don't go. I shan't practise now even if you do.
Mrs Dalmahoy Alex . . .
Alex I mean it!
Mrs Dalmahoy Right! If that's how you feel. I don't intend to bandy words with you in front of strangers. I'll speak to you later.

She sweeps off

Don So! The peasants are in revolt. Miss Finden to the guillotine!
Alex Even peasants have limits of endurance, Mr Peters.
Don So I see. (*Offering her a cigarette*) Do the peasants smoke?
Alex They aren't allowed to. It may spoil their voice.

He continues to hold out his cigarette case. She takes a cigarette

Thank you.

He lights it for her. She holds the cigarette awkwardly and after a few puffs she relapses into a fit of coughing

Don (*holding out an ash tray*) You've made your gesture. Now put it out.
Alex (*stubbing it out*) You knew I didn't want it?
Don Yes.
Alex Then why did you make me smoke it?
Don Would you rather stick pins in a wax image of her?
Alex If it would do any good. You must think I hate her.
Don Don't you?
Alex Not really. Only when I'm angry.
Don I don't blame you. I'd be livid at being forced to jump through paper hoops.
Alex Is that how you see me?
Don With a frilly skirt and a funny hat on.
Alex (*with a laugh*) I didn't know it was so obvious.
Don Even the back row of the gods would get the message. Why does she do it?
Alex She wants me to make the most of my life. To achieve something really rewarding.
Don Next act—performing parrots!
Alex You don't believe me?
Don Of course I believe you. But I don't believe her. That's her justification, not yours. But what's her real motive? Frustrated ambition or just pure sadism?
Alex She's a good singer. She wants me to be the same.
Don For private enjoyment?
Alex No, public. She's convinced I have a voice.
Don Everyone has.
Alex You don't think so?
Don I'm no judge. But it doesn't really matter what sort of voice you've got these days. The nearer it sounds to a nutmeg grater the higher you're likely to go in the Top Twenty. If that's what you want. But if you really want to sing . . .

Alex I don't.

Don Then what do you want?

Alex I don't know.

Don That's your trouble. If you did have a burning ambition to do something you wouldn't tolerate Mama's attempts to use you. I bet she wanted to be an opera star.

Alex You're right. She did.

Don What stopped her? Lack of talent?

Alex No. Her parents—and marriage.

Don What's the audition she's fixed for you?

Alex BBC. Next Monday afternoon.

Don I'd skip it if I were you. Give her the slip outside Broadcasting House or wherever it is.

Alex I couldn't do that.

Don Why not?

Alex Everyone knows. They'd think I'd funked it. At the last minute.

Don Ever thought of giving her the slip for good?

Alex (*quietly*) Yes.

Don What stopped you?

Alex I'd rather not talk about it.

Don OK. But you'll have to do without Mama sometime. You've thought about that I suppose?

Alex Please ...

Don (*picking up his book and making for the door*) All right. End of discussion.

Alex Don't go ... please ...

He hesitates. They look at each other in silence for a moment

Don Well?

Alex I ... I like talking to you. ... There's no-one here to talk to ...

Don You wouldn't say that if you'd spent the last half-hour in here. They've all done nothing but talk.

Alex That's different. I mean there's no-one to talk to about ... well about things that matter ... the girls at the shop only discuss boy-friends and clothes.

Don So you work in a shop?

Alex Whitesides—down the road.

Don But I thought you were only here on a visit. What was it Mama said? "We come here in the spring, we spend the summer in the country and we winter in France."

Alex She's quite right. We come here when the spring sales are on so I can get a job as a temporary sales assistant. We spend the summer in Bodmin helping out at my aunt's guest house and in winter we go to a small château outside Lyons owned by an old school-friend of my mother. I earn my keep there as a seamstress.

Don Do they know?

Alex Who?

Don The residents?

Alex No, I don't think so. She's ashamed to let them know. You know how it is.

Don I know. Keep them guessing. Give the impression you're too damn proud even to sit down with them at dinner.

Alex That's not pride.

Don Then what the hell is it?

Alex Poverty I suppose.

Don Poverty?

Alex We can't afford dinner. We eat sandwiches in her bedroom.

Don Oh my God, you're a queer one you are.

Alex Why?

Don You spend years building up an illusion of genteel affluence then shatter it all in front of a total stranger for no apparent reason. Why?

Alex It wasn't meant for you. It was meant for them. They expect it. They have their own illusions. You wouldn't have believed it anyway.

Don Maybe not. But I'd have respected it.

Alex I don't think so. I doubt very much whether you'd respect anything.

Don What is there to respect?

Alex Illusions. You just said so.

Don That was from one illusionist to another. Shatter them and there's nothing.

Alex You don't believe that.

Don I do. You and I represent the generation without future. How can we respect those responsible for that heritage? In ten years, maybe less, there'll be nothing.

Alex I'd hate to think you were right.

Don If I am at least we'll be spared the humiliation of dragging out the last years of our existence in a fifth-rate Bayswater hotel.

Alex That doesn't worry me.

Don Then you've thought about it?

Alex Of course I've thought about it. Seeing them all, day after day you can't help thinking about it. I'm half-way there already.

Don You've got to make a break. Get away.

Alex I can't.

Don You must.

Alex I can't leave her. I need her.

Don You don't. It's her that needs you.

Alex I couldn't live on my own.

Don You don't have to. Get out. Meet people. People your own age. You're young. Why you might even get married.

Alex (*laughing*) Married? Me?

Don I'm not laughing.

Alex Look at me! Just look at me!

Don I'm looking.

Alex Then what do you see? No, don't answer. I'll tell you. A spinster of thirty-five. No figure. Hair that's never seen a hairdresser. Clothes that don't fit right. Shy. Awkward. No charm. A fine bet for any man. No-one would look at me twice.

Don (*after a slight pause*) I would.

He moves to her and kisses her. After a second or two they part and she sits trembling

Alex (*softly*) You shouldn't have done that.
Don (*gently*) I'll nip out to Bernotti's. Get some wine. I won't be long. My room's on the third floor. Number thirty-three.

Don goes off

Alex remains seated trembling a little. She chokes back a sob

Mrs O'Neil enters, carrying her rug

Mrs O'Neil If I'd known they were going to kill him off in the first ten minutes I wouldn't have bothered to go and watch.

She realizes that Alex is not listening to her

Alex, are you all right?
Alex Yes. Yes I'm fine.
Mrs O'Neil You don't look it. You're trembling.
Alex I'm just cold. That's all. It's the stove. It's gone down.
Mrs O'Neil I'll get Mrs McEwan to make it up.
Alex No. No, don't bother.
Mrs O'Neil It's no bother.
Alex I'm not going to stay in. I want to go out.
Mrs O'Neil At this time?
Alex Take me out please.
Mrs O'Neil Me? Where, for heaven's sake?
Alex Anywhere. The cinema.
Mrs O'Neil The cinema? Well I suppose there is time to catch the last performance. But I generally go on Thursday afternoons. Pensioners' matinee. Half-price. Still if you really feel like it . . .
Alex I do.
Mrs O'Neil Right then. We'll go to the Odeon. There's a really good film on there. All about monsters from Outer Space. You'll love it. Come on. We'll need our coats.

They move to the door as—

the CURTAIN *falls*

SCENE 2

The same. The following afternoon. It is Saturday
Miss Fanner is asleep in the chair above the fireplace. Mrs O'Neil is busily engaged with her rug. After knotting in a few strands of wool, she puts her head on one side and looks appraisingly at her work. Then, to get a better effect, she spreads the rug on the floor and retreats a few paces. She backs into an

occasional table on which some books are stacked. They fall to the floor with a clatter. The noise wakes Miss Fanner

Miss Fanner Oh dear!

Mrs O'Neil It's all right. It's only me knocking the place down.

Miss Fanner I must have dropped off.

Mrs O'Neil You did. (*Still surveying her rug*) Och! I've gone wrong with that flower.

Miss Fanner I can't help it, you know.

Mrs O'Neil Can't help what, dear?

Miss Fanner Sleeping. After lunch. I've got so used to a siesta. After all those years.

Mrs O'Neil That must be it. Och! It's that last petal. I've made it too big. I'll just have to take some out.

Miss Fanner I dropped off in the Orangery the other day. But not for long. The seat was too uncomfortable.

Mrs O'Neil It'll mean wasting some of the magenta wool. And that'll make me short. Och well, I'll just have to get another ounce.

Miss Fanner I love the Orangery. It reminds me so much of my little room. With the orange tree outside. In summer you could smell the blossom all over the house.

Mrs O'Neil Just like the fish here on Fridays.

Mrs Dalmahoy enters and crosses to the piano where she starts to rummage through the pile of music and magazines on top of the piano

The others watch her. She gives a snort of exasperation

Lost something have you?

Mrs Dalmahoy My music. I left it here this morning. It seems to have gone.

Mrs O'Neil Have you asked Mrs McEwan about it?

Mrs Dalmahoy I've hardly had time. I've only just discovered it's missing.

Mrs O'Neil Then I'd ask her if I were you. She's probably put it away for safety.

Mrs Dalmahoy Perhaps. But she's never moved it before. And I've left it here on many occasions.

Mrs O'Neil What are you inferring? That one of us has pinched it?

Mrs Dalmahoy One can't trust anybody these days. Particularly the Irish.

Mrs O'Neil All right. I confess. I took two sheets upstairs before lunch. To line the bottom of me wardrobe. And Miss Fanner took one to wrap her fish and chips up in ...

Miss Fanner (*not wishing to become involved*) No, no I didn't. I never eat fish ...

Mrs Dalmahoy (*to Mrs O'Neil*) If that was meant to be a facetious reply ...

Mrs O'Neil Then it's a fitting answer to a malicious remark.

Mrs Dalmahoy The meaning of my remark was, I thought, quite clear. As you are quite capable of annoying me by taking my daughter out without my knowledge then you are equally capable of annoying me by deliberately hiding my music.

Mrs O'Neil Don't be so damn petty. If you took your daughter out a bit more she wouldn't ask other people to accompany her.

Mrs Dalmahoy I'm sure she never made such a suggestion.

Mrs O'Neil Are you now? And I suppose you're equally sure that she's adequately nourished. We called for a meal on the way back and she put away enough to feed a couple of farm labourers.

Mrs Dalmahoy I don't intend to indulge in a vulgar brawl on how to bring up my daughter. That is my affair.

Mrs O'Neil Then next time you pick a quarrel don't bring her into it.

Miss Fanner (*desperately trying to escape*) I ... er ... think I'll go and see Mrs McEwan. I haven't paid this week's account yet. I generally settle up with her on Saturday. (*She rises picking up the magazine in her lap. Two sheets of music fall out of the magazine on to the floor. She gazes at them in horror*) Oh dear!

Mrs Dalmahoy (*pouncing on the music sheets*) So! You didn't know where they were, eh?

Miss Fanner I had no idea ...

Mrs Dalmahoy Sitting there all along with them hidden away in a magazine.

Miss Fanner I didn't know ... really I didn't. I picked the magazine up from the top of the piano after lunch. They must have slipped inside it.

Mrs Dalmahoy A likely tale!

Mrs O'Neil On the contrary. An obvious explanation. Half the residents have been thumbing them magazines over since lunch time.

Mrs Dalmahoy I don't believe it was an accident. I believe it was done deliberately to annoy me. In the same way that she deliberately locks herself up in the bathroom every evening when she knows I want to fill my kettle.

Miss Fanner But I had no idea ...

Mrs Dalmahoy Then whom do you imagine rattles the door knob every night?

Miss Fanner I didn't know ... I'm sorry if I've caused you an inconvenience ...

Mrs O'Neil Och! Don't apologize to her. That's all she's wanting. To see you crawl. She's got a wash basin in her bedroom. She can fill it there.

Mrs Dalmahoy No I can't. The basin's too small to get the kettle under the tap.

Mrs O'Neil Then try filling it with a jug.

Miss Fanner (*seizing her opportunity to escape*) I really must go. Mrs McEwan will be expecting me. (*She crosses to the door and on her way nervously hands the music to Mrs Dalmahoy*) I'm sorry. I ...

Mrs Dalmahoy snatches the music from her

Miss Fanner scuttles quickly out of the room

There is a pause as Mrs Dalmahoy and Mrs O'Neil glare at each other in hostility. Then Mrs Dalmahoy crosses to the piano, sits on the stool and spreads the music out on the rest. Mrs O'Neil crosses to the radio. Mrs

Dalmahoy flexes her fingers and is about to strike a chord. Mrs O'Neil switches on the radio. Music blares forth. Mrs Dalmahoy swings round angrily on her stool

Mrs Dalmahoy You did that deliberately!
Mrs O'Neil What?
Mrs Dalmahoy Turned the radio on.
Mrs O'Neil Of course I did it deliberately. I didn't knock the switch on by me elbow in mistake.
Mrs Dalmahoy You did it deliberately because you saw I was going to play the piano.
Mrs O'Neil No. I did it deliberately to hear the three o'clock racing results.
Mrs Dalmahoy Would you please turn it off.
Mrs O'Neil (*turning the radio up louder*) What?
Mrs Dalmahoy The radio. Would you please turn it off.
Mrs O'Neil I can't hear what you're saying.
Mrs Dalmahoy I'm asking you to turn off the radio.
Mrs O'Neil The what?
Mrs Dalmahoy The radio!
Mrs O'Neil Why?
Mrs Dalmahoy Because we don't want to hear it!
Mrs O'Neil "We"? What do you mean "we"? Only Her Majesty the Queen and the editor of *The Times* can call themselves "we". Unless of course you happen to have a tape-worm!
Mrs Dalmahoy Oh!

In great indignation she slams down the piano lid, gets up and stalks off through the french windows into the garden

Mrs O'Neil switches off the radio in triumph and returns her attention to her rug

After a moment or two Alex enters. She looks round

Alex Oh, I thought Mother was in here.
Mrs O'Neil She was. But she's outside in the garden now. Cooling off.
Alex Cooling off?
Mrs O'Neil I've just insulted her. In return for all the insults she's been hurling at everyone else. Poor Miss Fanner couldn't take it. She scuttled out in terror not more than two minutes ago.
Alex I'm sorry.
Mrs O'Neil Sorry? Why should you be sorry?
Alex It's probably my fault. It's me she's really angry with.
Mrs O'Neil And what have you done? Apart, of course, from committing the Eighth Deadly Sin of sneaking off with me to the flicks?
Alex I've refused to attend the audition on Monday.
Mrs O'Neil You have? Well now, that is quite a step to take.
Alex You don't approve?
Mrs O'Neil I'm not one to sit in judgement, my dear. But I will say this. I love listening to your singing.

Alex You do?

Mrs O'Neil In fact I sometimes get up early and sneak down into the hall. Just to listen to you. Now you didn't know that, did you?

Alex No. I hadn't any idea.

Mrs O'Neil Mind you I'll be quite honest. I don't think you'll ever make the concert platform. But what does it matter. As long as you give pleasure to a few old fogies like myself you'll have achieved something.

Alex I wish she could see it that way. But she never will.

Don enters and overhears her next remark

She's far too ambitious for me.

Mrs O'Neil All mothers are ambitious for their daughters. Don't you agree, Mr Peters?

Don I don't know. I've never been a mother.

He looks at Alex. She turns away

How's the prayer mat coming on?

Mrs O'Neil Nearly finished. I'd lend it to you if I thought it would encourage you to get down on your knees a bit more.

Don Do that. I'll use it every night.

Mrs O'Neil For prayin'?

Don No. Looking through keyholes.

Mrs O'Neil Of course. I might have known. You're obviously that type.

Don You can always tell us by our eyes. One is more bloodshot than the other.

Mrs O'Neil Yours both look much the same to me.

Don That's because I'm out of practice. There aren't many keyholes in this establishment that I'd waste my time on.

Mrs O'Neil Then why waste your time in this establishment at all, Mr Peters?

Don Curiosity.

Mrs O'Neil To see how the other half lives?

Don And dies.

Mrs O'Neil Oh, they do that all right, Mr Peters. Generally in the lavatory. They're always having to break the door down. Let's hope it doesn't happen to you.

Don It won't. I'll have moved on long before then.

Mrs O'Neil To much bigger and better things no doubt. (*She looks at her watch*) Which reminds me. I must be moving too. To get more magenta. Before the shops shut.

Don Magenta?

Mrs O'Neil Wool, Mr Peters. To finish this flower on me prayer mat. You'll excuse me I hope?

Don Of course.

Mrs O'Neil collects her rug and wool together and moves to the door where she hesitates. She is uneasy as she senses that there is some kind of tension between Don and Alex. He is staring at her. She is avoiding his gaze

Mrs O'Neil Your mother's in the garden if you want her, Alex.
Alex Thank you. You did mention it.

Mrs O'Neil goes off

There is a pause. Don crosses to Alex

Don Well?

She turns and faces him

Why didn't you come? I waited for you. Till midnight.
Alex I went out.
Don You mean you ran away.
Alex Put it like that if you want.
Don But why?
Alex I don't know. I don't know why.
Don I do. You ran away because you always run away.
Alex That's not true.
Don Yes it is. You run away from decisions. You've never made one in your life. You let her make them all for you.
Alex Not any longer. I've made one today. A big decision.
Don Not to attend the audition?
Alex How did you know?
Don I thought you might.
Alex So you're wrong you see. I do make decisions.
Don Do you?
Alex Don't you believe me?
Don Oh, I believe you all right.
Alex But you don't believe I've told her?
Don I believe that as well. But you'll go all the same. When the time comes. (*A pause*) Won't you?
Alex (*after a moment's hesitation*) No.
Don Then prove it.
Alex How can I? Till next Monday?
Don You can prove it before then.
Alex How?
Don The bottle of wine's still waiting.
Alex (*turning away from him*) No.
Don (*going up to her and putting his hands on her shoulders*) You don't really mean that.
Alex Don't please! Don't touch me!
Don (*turning her round*) But you want me to. Don't you?
Alex I don't!
Don Then why are you trembling? (*He tries to kiss her*)
Alex (*turning her face away*) No. It's all wrong ...
Don What's wrong about it?
Alex Just to want someone ...
Don Why?
Alex Because with you there's nothing else ...

Don That's for tomorrow.

Alex There is no tomorrow . . . you said so . . . with you there's only today.

Don There's still tonight.

He kisses her. This time she does not resist. Her arms go round his neck

Miss Fanner (*off*) Mrs O'Neil!

Alex and Don break

Miss Fanner enters

Mrs O'Neil! . . . Oh, I'm sorry. I thought Mrs O'Neil was still here.

Don She's gone out.

Alex To buy wool for her rug. I don't think she'll be long.

Miss Fanner Oh dear. (*She sits in "her" chair*) I must talk to her. It's most important. Important for us all.

Alex What is?

Miss Fanner This. (*She holds up a letter*) I've just picked it up from the rack in the hall. There's one for each of us. Typewritten . . . so impersonal . . . she should have got us all together and explained . . .

Alex Who should?

Miss Fanner Miss McEwan. She's given us all notice to leave by the end of this month.

Mrs Dalmahoy enters from the garden

Alex Leave?

Miss Fanner The hotel's closing down.

Mrs Dalmahoy Rubbish!

Miss Fanner It's quite true. (*She holds up the letter*) I have it here in black and white.

Mrs Dalmahoy We have a reservation until the end of June. I have Mrs McEwan's confirmation in black and white.

Miss Fanner It says here that I must vacate my room by May the thirty-first.

Mrs Dalmahoy Obviously some misunderstanding. Unless of course she's decided to get rid of her unwelcome guests. Or those who don't settle their accounts promptly.

Alex Mother!

Miss Fanner You know very well that I pay my account regularly every week. Why I left you to pay it scarcely twenty minutes ago.

Mrs Dalmahoy You said that's what you were going to do. How do I know that you did?

Miss Fanner Do you want to see my receipt?

Mrs Dalmahoy I'm not really very interested. Come Alex . . . (*She moves to the door*)

The Colonel enters holding two letters in identical, typewritten envelopes. He hands one to Mrs Dalmahoy

Colonel For you Mrs Dalmahoy.

Mrs Dalmahoy For me?

Colonel It was in the rack. I noticed it as I was collecting mine. I heard you talking in here so I took the liberty of bringing it in to you. Mine is identical. We are all, I'm afraid, under notice to leave.

Mrs Dalmahoy (*ripping open the letter*) This is preposterous. I have a reservation . . .

Don To the end of June.

Mrs Dalmahoy Nearly two months. Mrs McEwan can't treat me like this! I shall sue her!

Don I wouldn't try.

Mrs Dalmahoy Why not?

Don Because a reservation does not constitute a legal agreement.

Mrs Dalmahoy That is a matter of opinion.

Don It's a matter of fact.

Mrs Dalmahoy I'm not interested in your advice, Mr Peters.

Don Then ask your lawyer. You'll get the same answer and pay through the nose for it.

Mrs Roski enters holding an identical envelope

Colonel I'm afraid he's right. There's nothing much we can do about it.

Mrs Dalmahoy Oh yes there is. We can at least demand an explanation from Mrs McEwan. (*She moves towards the door*)

Mrs Roski Vait! She is coming to see us. I 'ave just spoken to her in the hall.

Mrs Dalmahoy Did she say anything . . .?

Mrs Roski No, but she vill. I think she is as upset as we all are.

Miss Fanner Perhaps we can persuade her to give us a little more time. I'll be back in Spain in a few months . . . And you Colonel. You may well be back in Surrey . . .

Colonel Unlikely.

Miss Fanner But your wife's improving. You said she was much better when you saw her last Sunday . . .

Colonel It's the spring. She always gets better in the spring.

Miss Fanner I think we should ask her to delay giving notice for at least six months.

Colonel We can try.

Mrs Roski She is a fair woman. If she can do it she vill. If she cannot then ve vill just 'ave to look for somewhere else.

Colonel And that certainly won't be easy.

Mrs Roski Similar accommodation on the same terms vill be impossible.

Colonel Of course. You've tried before.

Mrs Roski Many times. For the sake of my stomach. But no place I 'ave seen compares with this in price. So for reasons of economics I put up with indigestion.

Colonel She's been very reasonable. The increase in her terms over the years has been minimal.

Miss Fanner Perhaps that's why she's closing. Perhaps she can't afford to run the place any longer.

Colonel If that is the case then perhaps we could all do something about it.

Mrs Dalmahoy I certainly wouldn't be prepared to pay more for the accommodation I'm getting here.
Colonel What about you, Mrs Roski?
Mrs Roski It vill take me longer to save for my passage to America.
Colonel Then your answer is no?
Mrs Roski My stomach says no. But my 'ead says yes.
Colonel Miss Fanner?
Miss Fanner I could manage to pay a little more. But it depends on how much. I can cut out the cinema and cancel my magazines. I can always read them in the library . . .
Colonel Mr Peters?
Don I'm not a permanent resident.
Colonel Then it won't concern you. If you're all agreeable I'm prepared to tell Mrs McEwan that if finance is the problem then most of us, including myself, would be prepared to pay a little more for our accommodation . . .

The door opens

Mrs Roski She's here now . . .

They all turn expectantly to the door

Mrs O'Neil enters and stops short in surprise

Mrs O'Neil (*looking from one to the other*) Well? What are you all staring at? Have I got me dress on back to front?
Miss Fanner We thought you were Mrs McEwan.
Mrs O'Neil And what's Mrs McEwan done wrong?
Mrs Roski Expelled us.
Colonel We've all had a letter . . .
Mrs O'Neil (*fumbling in her handbag and bringing out a letter*) Is this it?
Colonel It looks like it.
Mrs O'Neil (*opening it*) It was in the rack when I went out. I just slipped it in me bag. I thought it was me bill. (*She reads it*) Well I suppose we could always put up a marquee in Hyde Park.
Mrs Dalmahoy That's not very funny.
Mrs O'Neil But it's practical. You wouldn't need to queue for the bathroom. You could fill your kettle in the Serpentine.

Mrs Dalmahoy gives a snort of disgust and turns away

Colonel We're thinking of asking Mrs McEwan for longer notice.
Mrs O'Neil How long?
Colonel A few months.
Miss Fanner Until I go to Spain and your daughter comes back from India.
Mrs O'Neil And if that's not possible?
Mrs Roski We vill probably 'ave to look for somewhere else.
Mrs Dalmahoy That's no problem as far as I'm concerned. My daughter and I will simply go to our summer residence a little earlier than usual.
Colonel Alternatively, if finance is Mrs McEwan's problem, we might all offer to pay her a little more for our accommodation. Would you support such a proposition?

Mrs O'Neil Of course I would. I'm not quite a pauper yet. Even though I've no summer residence to go to.

Colonel Good. Then I'll put that proposition to her.

Mrs McEwan enters, carrying a letter

All eyes are upon her. There is a pause

Mrs McEwan First I'd like to say how sorry I am. The letter I've just sent you all must have come as a very great shock. All I can say is that I share the feeling. Pulling up roots and starting afresh after thirty years isn't going to be easy for me either. I would love to keep the hotel going but unfortunately that just isn't possible . . .

Colonel If it's a question of finance a number of us would be willing to pay more . . .

Mrs McEwan That's a very kind offer but I'm afraid it does not alter the situation, Colonel.

Colonel Is there any chance of extending the date . . .?

Mrs McEwan I'm afraid not.

Colonel But it's such short notice. A few more months would help us all considerably . . .

Mrs McEwan I'm sorry.

Colonel But surely you must have known all about this for some time. Couldn't you have warned us months ago?

Mrs McEwan I could.

Mrs Roski Then vy did you not do so?

Mrs McEwan Because I'd hoped to avoid closure. I've been negotiating with the new lessees for over a year for an extension of my tenancy. Yesterday, however, I received a letter from them regretting that an extension beyond the end of June could not be granted.

Mrs Roski So the hotel is no longer yours?

Mrs McEwan It never was mine. I had it on a thirty years' lease which expires in three weeks' time.

Mrs Roski And who are these new lessees?

Mrs McEwan They call themselves the Venture Property Company.

Mrs O'Neil And what are they going to do with it now they've got it? Pull it down and stick up one of those matchbox-on-end abortions?

Don They certainly would—if the Planning Authority would let them.

Mrs O'Neil And what do you know about it?

Don A lot. I work for them.

Mrs O'Neil The Planning Authority?

Don No. The Venture Property Company. I'm their Chief Designer.

With the exception of Mrs McEwan they all look at him in astonishment

Colonel Then you've known all along . . .

Miss Fanner And never mentioned it . . .

Mrs Roski A fifth columnist! Sent here to spy on us!

Don Now, wait a minute. Let's get things in perspective. I'm a paying guest. Just as you all are. I get no special privileges . . .

Colonel But you're here for a purpose.

Don I need temporary accommodation. That's the only difference between us. You're all here for good.

Miss Fanner That's quite untrue, Mr Peters. We're only here temporarily ourselves. Colonel Blanchard's going back to Surrey, Mrs Roski's going to America ...

Don And you're going to Spain.

Miss Fanner As soon as the invitation arrives.

Mrs McEwan Which reminds me. This is probably it. (*She holds out the letter*) It was posted in Seville.

Miss Fanner For me?

Mrs McEwan I'm awfully sorry. I should have given it to you when I came in. It arrived this morning. It must have slipped out of the letter rack. I spotted it just now behind the hat-stand as I came across the hall.

Miss Fanner Thank you. (*She takes the letter*) Which I think proves my point rather well, Mr Peters.

Don Does it? I wonder.

Colonel I'm wondering too, Mr Peters. I'm still unconvinced that your stay here is not connected with your firm's interest in this hotel.

Mrs Roski I agree. It is too much of a coincidence.

Colonel Why, for example, did you choose to stay here when there are hundreds of other hotels you could have gone to?

Mrs O'Neil What made you come? To see us all in trouble?

Alex Or to offer us hope?

Mrs O'Neil Well, Mr Peters?

Don looks at Alex. She returns his gaze, challenging him to answer

Don The answer's quite simple. I came here to save time.

Mrs O'Neil To save time?

Don By ensuring that the plans I have drawn up can be put into operation immediately on the first of July.

Colonel Plans? What plans?

Don The conversion plans. You don't imagine my firm is taking this place over in order to preserve it, do you?

Colonel But you've already said that the Planning Authority won't let you demolish.

Don Not demolish, Colonel, reconstruct. On the first of July the contractors are due to move in. They'll gut the place. Staircase, fireplaces and cracked lavatory pans. The lot. They'll all go.

Colonel And ... ?

Don Then they'll build. Plate glass, natural wood, flush doors, fluorescent lights, fitted carpets and the very latest in Continental wallpaper. End result ... flatlets.

Mrs O'Neil (*in disgust*) Flatlets?

Don For the business man, the single lady and the retired couple. All complete with electric cooker, folding bed, television, refuse destructor, constant hot water and communal launderette.

Mrs O'Neil And not enough room in which to swing a cat around!

Don No pets allowed.

Colonel So that's what we've got to make room for.

Don Can't stop progress, Colonel.

Mrs Roski Progress? Is that what you call progress?

Don What else?

Mrs Roski It depends what you mean by progress.

Don In this case it means more efficient use of available space. When the conversion's complete this place will hold treble the number of residents. And you realize what that means ...

Mrs O'Neil Treble the profit.

Don I'm serious. Just think what it'll mean to the community as a whole. A reduction in commuters, the easing of pressure on public transport, less call for development on the connurbation fringe ...

Alex And a handful of old people with nowhere to go.

There is a pause

Don That's just where you're wrong. The human problems that progress creates can't be ignored. My firm realizes that. That's why we're prepared to offer assistance to anyone in difficulty.

Colonel Assistance? What sort of assistance?

Don Alternative accommodation.

Colonel Here?

Don Why not?

Colonel But good God man why didn't you say so before?

Don I never got the chance.

Miss Fanner Then we don't have to move after all?

Don Only temporarily. Whilst the conversion takes place.

There is an outburst of relief from everyone. Comments such as "Thank goodness for that", "What a relief", "He should have said so before" are heard simultaneously

Alex Just a minute!

There is sudden silence

Let him finish his story.

Don Finish?

Alex Go on. Tell them the rest.

Don The rest?

Alex The price they'll be expected to pay for a flatlet.

Don Well, the Company's a private organization and not eligible for subsidy like Local Authorities. Nevertheless, it has decided to charge ten per cent less than the economic rent to any resident who wishes to stay.

Colonel Which amounts to?

Don Sixty pounds a week.

There is a stunned silence

Mrs McEwan I'm sorry. This is out of my hands. You'll no doubt wish to talk it over. I ... I must go and supervize the dinner ...

Mrs McEwan exits

Mrs Roski Sixty pounds!

Mrs O'Neil With no board!

Don It includes heating and lighting.

Mrs Dalmahoy Robbery! Daylight robbery! Not that it concerns me. My daughter and I are leaving this place anyway. Come Alex. We must dress for dinner.

Mrs Dalmahoy goes off followed by Alex

Colonel I'm afraid this is rather more than I anticipated.

Don I'm sorry. But those are the Company's terms. I have no power to adjust them. (*A pause*) You'll wish to think it over of course.

Colonel Naturally.

Don Though you'll appreciate that I cannot wait indefinitely for a decision.

Colonel Of course.

Don I would add that conversions of this nature generally attract a long waiting list of prospective tenants.

Colonel How long have we got to make up our minds?

Don A week. I would like a decision from all of you by next Saturday. Now I'm sure you'll wish to talk it over.

Don exits

Colonel Well?

Mrs O'Neil As far as I'm concerned he can stuff his flatlets. I wouldn't stay here even if I could afford it. Which I can't.

Colonel My feelings are very much the same.

Mrs Roski Tomorrow I vill start my search for new accommodation again.

Miss Fanner With food to buy as well it would be quite impossible for me.

Mrs O'Neil What are you worrying about? You'll be off to Spain before they start knocking the place about.

Miss Fanner My letter! Of course! I'd quite forgotten. Do please excuse me while I read it. (*She opens the letter and starts to read*)

Mrs Roski There's a place in Hereford Road I looked at two months ago. It vas not much dearer than this.

Mrs O'Neil Then why didn't you take it?

Mrs Roski It smelt of cats!

Mrs O'Neil Couldn't be worse than the cabbage in this place.

Mrs Roski It was. Cabbage is edible There vos also a place in Prince's Square. On the corner. Now that is a possibility.

Mrs O'Neil Then why did you give it a miss?

Mrs Roski No evening meal.

Mrs O'Neil If the terms are all right you can always cut yourself a sandwich in the bedroom. Don't you agree, Colonel?

Colonel I'd miss my dinner. Always been used to it. Dressed for it too when I first came here. Till my dinner jacket wore out.

Mrs O'Neil That Mrs Dalmahoy does just the opposite.

Colonel Opposite? Opposite to what?

Mrs O'Neil Opposite to you. She still dresses but she's given up dinner.

They are suddenly aware that Miss Fanner has finished reading her letter and is sitting motionless staring into space

Well dear, when do you go?

Miss Fanner Go?

Mrs O'Neil To Spain.

Miss Fanner (*appearing bewildered*) There must be some mistake.

Mrs O'Neil Mistake? Don't tell us you've opened someone else's letter.

Miss Fanner No ... no the letter's for me. It's for me all right.

Mrs O'Neil (*becoming suddenly concerned*) What's the matter dear? Is something wrong?

Miss Fanner (*softly*) They don't want me.

Mrs O'Neil Who doesn't?

Miss Fanner They don't want me any more.

Mrs O'Neil Who? Carlos and his wife?

Miss Fanner They think I'm too old.

Mrs O'Neil exchanges glances with Mrs Roski and the Colonel

Mrs O'Neil Don't you think you ought to go to your room and have a little lie down, dear?

Miss Fanner No. No, I'm perfectly all right.

Mrs O'Neil (*going to her*) Come on, dear. I'll go up with you.

She helps Miss Fanner to her feet

Miss Fanner Maybe they're right. It's never occurred to me. Maybe I am too old.

Mrs O'Neil Of course you're not.

Miss Fanner It'll take a long time ...

Mrs O'Neil What will, dear?

Miss Fanner Getting used to the idea ... of someone else ... in my little room ... I'll miss the orange tree ...

Mrs O'Neil Och! Who cares about an old orange tree. You've still got your azalea. It's a mass of bloom at the moment. The prize of the garden!

Miss Fanner I haven't seen it today.

Mrs O'Neil Go and have a look. Cheer yourself up. Go on now.

Miss Fanner hesitates a moment, gives a wan smile and nods

Miss Fanner I will.

She goes off into the garden

Mrs O'Neil I've been afraid of this all along. She'd so set her heart on going back.

Mrs Roski None of us can go back.

Colonel But we all try.

Mrs Roski And learn.

Colonel It took me a long time.

Miss Fanner appears at the french windows. She is holding her azalea plant which is crushed and broken

Mrs O'Neil What's she doing?

She goes quickly to the french windows and opens them. Miss Fanner enters slowly

You've plucked it! What have you plucked it for?

Miss Fanner I didn't ... it's broken ... someone's broken it.

Mrs O'Neil It was growing fine when I went out there after lunch. No-one's been out there since—(*She breaks off remembering her quarrel with Mrs Dalmahoy*)

Miss Fanner Must put it in water ... It might live ... for a bit ...

Miss Fanner goes off slowly

The others watch her

Mrs O'Neil That Mrs-bloody-Dalmahoy! The rotten spiteful bitch!

CURTAIN

ACT II

SCENE 1

The same. Later that same evening

When the CURTAIN *rises Don is sitting at the desk* DL. *Mrs McEwan is standing beside him. He is scanning a document which she has given him. She is waiting for him to finish reading it and then comment on it*

Don (*putting the document down and shaking his head*) I'm sorry. There's nothing. Not a thing.

Mrs McEwan Not even the Vent-Axia fans?

Don We won't need them. Not with air-conditioning. They're out-of-date in any case.

Mrs McEwan I wondered about the bed linen as the flatlets will be fully-furnished ...

Don The first tenants will expect everything to be new ... fresh ... and attractive. We can't spoil the image with a lot of second-hand junk ...

Mrs McEwan (*picking up the document*) I see. (*She moves to the door*)

Don Aren't you keeping anything yourself?

Mrs McEwan A few personal things ... that's all.

Don No ideas about starting up somewhere else?

Mrs McEwan It's a bit late in the day for me ...

Don What will you do? Retire?

Mrs McEwan I don't know yet. I'll spend a few months with a married sister down at Worthing. After that ... (*She shrugs*)

Don We'll need a permanent caretaker here when we're in business.

Mrs McEwan (*giving a short incredulous laugh*) Are you offering me a job?

Don The post hasn't been advertised yet. But the Board would accept my recommendation.

Mrs McEwan No thanks. I wouldn't want to stay here anyway. Not after you've converted the place.

Don So you're a sentimentalist.

Mrs McEwan I don't think so. Unless growing fond of a place is being sentimental. I've been here a long time. Since I was thirty. It's been my home, my place of work, my life. You can't see all that disappear without feeling something.

Don It won't disappear. It'll change. That's all.

Mrs McEwan I don't want to be here when it does.

Don But it'll be a change for the better.

Mrs McEwan That's a matter of opinion.

Don Or prejudice.

Mrs McEwan I don't agree.

Don But look what we're doing ...

Mrs McEwan You're making it pay.

Don Granted. But we're also making it bright, attractive and comfortable. With every modern convenience.

Mrs McEwan At the flick of a switch?

Don As far as possible.

Mrs McEwan Except for one thing ...

Don You name it. We'll lay it on.

Mrs McEwan You couldn't.

Don Go on. Try me.

Mrs McEwan There'd be no point. You wouldn't understand. We speak different languages. And belong to different worlds.

Don My world is today.

Mrs McEwan And mine is yesterday. So you have that advantage. (*She turns to go*)

Don Wait a minute!

Mrs McEwan (*turning*) Why?

Don You can't go like that. With a big question mark left hanging in the air. I don't like question marks. They're disturbing.

Mrs McEwan You surprise me. I thought nothing disturbed you, Mr Peters. You always appear to be so sure of yourself. And so sure that this new creation of yours will be perfect ...

Don It will be. By today's standards.

Mrs McEwan Then nothing I can say is likely to alter your conviction.

Don I'm willing to listen.

Mrs McEwan You can't just put people into little gadget-filled boxes and expect them to be happy.

Don Why not?

Mrs McEwan Because they're human beings. They want to belong. To each other.

Don You're not serious.

Mrs McEwan I certainly am. I've watched them at close quarters for thirty years. This dusty old place with all its short-comings has far more to offer than the grand sterile honey-comb you want to put in its place.

Don (*with a touch of sarcasm*) You mean you gave them a home.

Mrs McEwan No. I couldn't do that. I gave them the next best thing. I gave them somewhere to meet and talk, to argue and bore each other stiff. A place where they could communicate with other human beings. A place where they weren't alone.

Don The plans do provide for a communal centre in the basement. For evening use.

Mrs McEwan And that solves the problem?

Don Why not?

Mrs McEwan They'd never use it.

Don Now you're contradicting yourself.

Mrs McEwan No I'm not. Human relationships can't just be turned on and off like a tap. It's no good keeping people in solitary confinement and then letting them loose at specified times like so many tame rabbits to meet their fellow creatures. They'd be embarrassed. Particularly when the place is blatantly labelled for that purpose. No. The contact must be subtle and gradual and there all the time. At the breakfast table, in the lounge after dinner, in the garden. Even in the queue for the bathroom. I could provide all that. You've nothing to replace it.

Don That's a matter of opinion.

Mrs McEwan Most things are.

Don Well, it looks as though I've driven your rabbits underground this evening. I've had this room to myself ever since dinner.

Mrs McEwan I think they're all out. Except Miss Fanner. You've really upset her. She didn't come down to dinner. I'll have to take her something up on a tray.

Alex enters

Hello Alex. I thought you were out.

Alex I've just come in.

Mrs McEwan With your mother?

Alex No. She's at the concert in the town hall.

Mrs McEwan She'll enjoy that. Good-night.

Mrs McEwan goes off

Alex Good-night.

Don Why didn't you go with her?

Alex I did. But I came out at the interval.

Don Didn't she object?

Alex What do you think?

Don You're having quite a day, aren't you?

Alex I've disagreed with her twice today. That's all.

Don And twice with me. In front of everyone else.

Alex I challenged you, yes. Someone had to speak up for them.

Don I was only doing my job.

Alex Some job! Kicking a handful of old pensioners out on to the street!

Don That's unfair. They don't have to go. They can stay here if they want.

Alex You mean if they can pay.

Don The choice is theirs.

Alex You know very well they can't pay.

Don How do I know that?

Alex Would they live here if they could?

Don That doesn't prove a thing. For all I know they may well have fat little nest eggs sewn up in their mattresses all ready to leave to some bloody cats' home.

Alex You don't believe that any more than I do.

Don Oh, for God's sake, Alex, stop preaching! What do you expect me to do? Tell them they can all stay on here for a pittance? If I went back to my firm with a deal like that I'd be out on my neck tomorrow.

Alex With a clear conscience.

Don You can't have a conscience in business.

Alex So you grab what you can today because there is no tomorrow. That's what you said isn't it? The generation without future.

Don Don't twist my words!

Alex Even if you're right and there is no tomorrow it still doesn't make sense. At the end of it all what will you have proved?

Don God knows. Success, I suppose.

Alex Success! (*She laughs*) That's a fine thing to prove! A great achievement to comfort you as you whirl into oblivion! (*She turns towards the door*)

Don Alex!

She pauses

Don't go! Please!

There is a pause

Tell me what I should do.

Alex (*moving back to him*) I can't tell you that. You've got to make up your own mind. Work it out for yourself.

Don But I can't throw everything away. Not now. Not with a junior partnership in sight.

Alex Is that so very important?

Don To me it is. To the miserable bewildered kid who was kicked out of his home by a bastard of a step-father. On his sixteenth birthday.

Alex Don!

Don Help me, please!

Alex I can't.

Don You can. (*He takes her in his arms and kisses her*)

Alex Don ... don't! It won't help.

Don It will. (*He kisses her again*) Let's go to my room.

Alex No.

Don Please. You promised.

Alex We mustn't be seen. Both going up together.

Don You go first. (*He hands her a key*) Here's my key. I'll pick up my papers and follow ...

Alex No Don, I ...

Don Go on. (*He gives her an affectionate peck on the cheek*) Light the candles ...

She gives him a wistful, uncertain smile and goes off

Don crosses to the desk and gathers his papers together. He starts to push them all into his briefcase

Mrs O'Neil enters

Mrs O'Neil Good-evening.

Don Oh. Good-evening.

Mrs O'Neil (*nodding at the papers*) Been doing your homework?

Don Homework? Oh, yes.

Mrs O'Neil Don't let me drive you out. I've only come in for a quick warm of my feet before going to bed. Didn't need to when I had a husband. Have you got the conversion plans in that case?

Don Why yes ... I ...

Mrs O'Neil Don't worry. I don't want to look at them. But I think it might be a good idea if you did.

Don Me?

Mrs O'Neil Yes you. Go through them again with a fine toothcomb. See if you can't make a few economies here and there. Then perhaps you might be able to offer us all accommodation at a reasonable price.

Don Sixty pounds a week for a flat in London is a very modest sum.

Mrs O'Neil Modest? I call it indecent.

Don That's hardly fair. The firm has made a gesture ...

Mrs O'Neil It has indeed. A couple of figures stuck up in the air!

The Colonel and Mrs Roski enter

Here's the Colonel and Mrs Roski. They got your message all right. They've been out all evening searching for alternative accommodation. Any luck, Colonel?

Colonel (*glaring at Don*) Very promising. Very promising indeed. I don't think it's going to be as difficult as we thought.

Don Then I assume you'll not be interested in the offer I made you this afternoon?

Colonel I think that's a reasonable assumption, Mr Peters.

Don looks at Mrs Roski for confirmation

Mrs Roski Most reasonable.

Don looks at Mrs O'Neil

Mrs O'Neil Don't look at me. I've nothing to add.

Don Then I'll say good-night. (*He moves to the door and hesitates*)

The others remain silent, ignoring him

Don exits

Mrs O'Neil Now tell me the truth.

Colonel Not much luck, I'm afraid.

Mrs Roski Ve 'ave tried five places.

Colonel It isn't only cost that's the problem. Most of them don't seem to have any vacancies.

Mrs Roski Except that one in Ladbroke Grove.

Mrs O'Neil (*in distaste*) Ladbroke Grove!

Colonel Not the most salubrious of neighbourhoods, I'm afraid, but ...

Mrs O'Neil I know. Beggars can't be choosers.

Colonel Their terms are higher than here.

Mrs Roski But they had six vacancies.

Colonel Provided you're willing to share a bedroom.

Mrs Roski Ve vill just 'ave to try again tomorrow.

Mrs O'Neil And I'll come with you.

Mrs McEwan enters. She carries a tray. On it is a plate of sandwiches and a glass of milk

Mrs McEwan Have any of you see Miss Fanner?
Mrs O'Neil She's not been in here.
Mrs McEwan I thought I'd take this up to her as she didn't come down for dinner.
Colonel Is she not in her room?
Mrs McEwan I'm not sure. I've just been up there. Her light wasn't on. I knocked once or twice but she didn't answer.
Colonel Did you try her door?
Mrs McEwan It's locked.
Colonel She's probably gone out.
Mrs McEwan That's what I thought. But I've just seen her umbrella in the hall stand. She doesn't usually go out without it.
Mrs O'Neil Och, she'll have fallen asleep.
Mrs McEwan That could very well be the explanation . . . although . . .
Colonel You are not sure?
Mrs McEwan No.
Mrs Roski Vy?
Mrs McEwan It's so unlike her. I've never known her miss dinner before. Or lock herself in her room. I'd feel happier if I knew for certain that she was all right.
Colonel You have a pass key to her room?
Mrs McEwan Yes, of course.
Colonel Then get it and I'll go along with you.
Mrs McEwan Oh, thank you, Colonel. It's very kind of you.
Colonel Not at all. If you're worried it's the only thing to do.

The Colonel and Mrs McEwan go off

Mrs Roski Mrs McEwan is a good woman. She takes her responsibilities very seriously.
Mrs O'Neil She has to. As proprietress. It's all part of her job. Making sure her guests are all right. After all most of us are knocking on in years. Folk of our age don't last for ever. I've seen quite a few go since I've been in this place.
Mrs Roski You mean die?
Mrs O'Neil Or take ill. The last was old Mr Loupenski. About three years ago. He collapsed in the lavatory on the second floor just after breakfast. When everyone was wanting to go.
Mrs Roski A heart attack?
Mrs O'Neil That's right. It took them an hour to get him out.
Mrs Roski I did not know this.
Mrs O'Neil It was before your time. Nice little man he was. But he had a terrible wife. She never stopped shouting at him. Or so he said. I never met her. He kept running away from her. That's why he came here. But the stroke finished him.
Mrs Roski How sad. To die like that.
Mrs O'Neil Oh, he didn't die. He went back to her. Paralysed. He couldn't run away any more after that.

The Colonel enters. He appears tense and worried

Colonel I wonder if you could give me a hand.
Mrs O'Neil Both of us?
Colonel Please.
Mrs O'Neil Miss Fanner?
Colonel Yes. She's tried to kill herself.
Mrs O'Neil Oh my God!

CURTAIN

SCENE 2

The same. Two days later. Early afternoon

It is a dull day. Rain is falling outside the window. Mrs O'Neil is sitting on the settee working on her rug, which is very nearly finished. Mrs Dalmahoy is sitting in the chair above the fireplace, reading. The Colonel is standing at the french windows looking out into the garden

Colonel There's no sign of a break yet. Damned weather. It looks as though it could go on for hours.
Mrs O'Neil It's the constant dripping from that broken gutter that gets on my nerves.
Colonel Let's hope it'll stop before three. The weatherman on the radio forecast a clearance from the west by mid-afternoon.
Mrs O'Neil Oh, I never trust them fellows. Me corn's much more reliable.
Colonel What's it doing now?
Mrs O'Neil Not throbbing as much as it did before lunch.
Colonel That's a good sign. Looks as though you and the weatherman might agree for once.
Mrs O'Neil Pure coincidence.
Colonel Well let's hope you're both right. It'll be miserable for her. Coming back in the rain.
Mrs Dalmahoy Why? She's not walking. I thought you'd arranged for a taxi to pick her up at the hospital.
Colonel I have.
Mrs Dalmahoy Then why worry about the weather?
Colonel Because the weather affects people.
Mrs Dalmahoy Rubbish.
Mrs O'Neil Of course it does. I always feel more on top of the world when it's a fine sunny day.
Mrs Dalmahoy It never affects me. People make or mar my day much more effectively. So if she's like me she'll be feeling far more worried about facing all of us again than making her entrance in a mackintosh.
Mrs O'Neil I'd have thought that some of us ought to be feeling much more apprehensive than her.
Mrs Dalmahoy And what do you mean by that?
Mrs O'Neil Those of us that have a conscience.

Mrs Dalmahoy And just what are you insinuating? That I am in some way responsible for her attempted suicide?

Mrs O'Neil I wouldn't say you were exactly responsible.

Mrs Dalmahoy I should hope not.

Mrs O'Neil But I reckon you helped it along.

Mrs Dalmahoy That's an outrageous suggestion!

Mrs O'Neil No more outrageous than what you did. Smashing down her azalea.

Mrs Dalmahoy A trivial matter like that!

Mrs O'Neil So it was you! I thought as much!

Mrs Dalmahoy No-one in their right senses would swallow a bottle of sleeping tablets over a stupid plant.

Mrs O'Neil She wasn't in her right senses at the time. She was suffering from shock.

Mrs Dalmahoy Shock?

Mrs O'Neil Shock and disappointment at opening a letter and finding she wasn't wanted any more.

Mrs Dalmahoy I wasn't to know that. I can't be held responsible for her inability to face up to reality. Just because she's weak——

Mrs O'Neil And timid and wouldn't retaliate. That's why you did it.

Mrs Dalmahoy Rubbish!

Mrs O'Neil Then why didn't you do it to me?

Mrs Dalmahoy Do what to you?

Mrs O'Neil Smash down my lilies. You were far more angry with me at the time than you were with her.

Mrs Dalmahoy My quarrel was with her. She had hidden my music. Not you.

Mrs O'Neil Och, come off it. You accused us both of hiding it. You didn't do it to me because you know full well I don't give a damn whether me lilies survive or not. You did it to her because you knew her azalea was important to her. Apart from Spain and the sunken garden it's the only thing she ever talks about. You may think that destroying it is a trivial matter. I think it's one of the worst things you could have done to her. And if you've any sort of conscience I hope it troubles you for the rest of your life!

Colonel Ladies! Please! What's done is done. We must all try and forget that it happened.

Mrs O'Neil I'll not forget.

Mrs Dalmahoy And I certainly won't!

She marches out of the room

Mrs O'Neil (*a little sheepishly*) Did I lay it on too thick?

Colonel (*smiling*) A bit.

Mrs O'Neil I had to get it off my chest.

Colonel It won't do her any harm.

Mrs O'Neil But will it do her any good?

Colonel It might. Her face was a picture when you gave her that last mouthful.

Mrs O'Neil Sorry about that. It's the Irish in me. Once I get going me tongue runs away with me.

Don enters, carrying his briefcase. He stops short on seeing them

Don Oh. Good-afternoon.
Colonel Good-afternoon.

Don moves to the desk and takes a plan, a pocket calculator, a tape measure, a notebook and pencil out of his briefcase. He crosses to the french windows, measures the depth and makes an entry in his notebook. The Colonel and Mrs O'Neil watch him curiously

Don Sorry to be a nuisance. I'm just checking up on a few measurements. Last minute change in the plans.
Colonel Are you going to be long?
Don Five minutes or so.
Colonel No longer I hope. We're having rather an important meeting in here shortly.
Don A meeting?
Colonel Well ... not exactly a meeting. More of a welcoming home party. For Miss Fanner.
Don Oh, I see. So it's today?
Colonel (*looking at his watch*) Yes. Any minute now. We're just waiting for her taxi to arrive. The hospital should have discharged her ten minutes ago.
Don Is she fully recovered?
Colonel Completely. I think they only kept her in an extra day just to make sure. Because of her age.
Don Well don't worry. I'll clear out when she comes.
Colonel (*to Mrs O'Neil*) I think it would be as well if we went into the dining-room and watched for the taxi from there.
Mrs O'Neil Good idea. It'll give us a bit of warning.
Colonel (*to Don*) As soon as it pulls up outside I'll let you know. Then you can clear off if you haven't finished what you're doing.
Don Right.

The Colonel and Mrs O'Neil go off. Mrs O'Neil takes her rug and wool with her

Don measures the width of the french windows and makes an entry in his notebook. He opens the french windows, looks out at the rain and hesitates

Alex enters. She has made a pathetic attempt to improve her appearance

Ah! You're just in time. Hang on to the end of this tape for me.

She hesitates

Come on!

She goes to him and takes the end of the tape. He puts up his collar and runs out into the garden. Within seconds he is back, slamming the french windows behind him

God! It's bloody wet out there! (*He puts his collar down, retracts the tape into its case, makes an entry in his notebook then crosses to the desk and sits. He does a calculation on his calculator and then takes a scale out of his briefcase and starts measuring a distance on the plan*)

Alex (*going to him*) What are you doing?

Don (*preoccupied*) Checking up some dimensions. And altering the plans. We're going to add a children's playroom. Build it where the garden is.

Hesitantly, she slips an arm round his shoulder and kisses the top of his head

Not now. I'm trying to work.

Alex Sorry. (*Her hand remains on his shoulder*)

Don Please. I've only got a few minutes to get this done.

Alex (*withdrawing her hand*) Is it so very urgent?

Don Yes, as a matter of fact it is.

Alex I haven't seen you since . . . I looked for you yesterday and this morning . . .

Don I've been busy. Round at the company office most of the time.

Alex Last night as well?

Don Look, I'll see you again tonight. OK? (*Turning to his papers*) Now will you please let me get on?

Alex Promise?

Don Of course I promise.

Alex You won't keep it. You'll go out again. Like you did last night.

Don (*throwing down his pencil*) Oh for Christ's sake! What is this? An inquisition? Can't I go anywhere without you spying on me?

Alex I'm not spying on you.

Don Then leave me alone. Stop behaving like a possessive bride.

She turns away from him, choking back the tears

I'm sorry Alex. Don't please. Someone might come in.

She controls herself with difficulty

Here! (*He hands her his handkerchief*) Now tell me what it is you want to say.

Alex I want to know where I stand. What to expect. I can't bear uncertainty.

Don Nothing's certain. For any of us.

Alex There was certainty for me. Before you came. An annual routine. Selling stockings in a shop, washing dishes in a guest house, sewing clothes in a French château.

Don Then back again to the stockings.

Alex Year after year . . .

Don It's still there. You can go back to it.

Alex But I don't want to. Don't you see what you've done? You've shown me another world. A world which I'd given up hope of ever reaching. I can't bear the thought of you shutting the door on it.

Don But you've known from the beginning . . .

Alex I've changed since the beginning. I hoped you had too . . .

Don Look, we can't discuss this now ...

Alex We must. I want to know now.

Don Want to know what? Whether you mean anything to me or not? Is that what you're after?

Alex I don't even want to know that. All I want to know is that I'll see you again ... sometimes ... just occasionally ... Nothing permanent ...

Don There couldn't be anything permanent. I'm married already.

Alex I know.

Don How did you know?

Alex I just guessed. Did she leave you?

Don No. I left her. But I'm going back to her.

Alex When?

Don At the end of the week.

Alex I see.

Don I'd no choice in the matter. She's the senior partner's daughter. And the eldest boy's been in trouble. With the police. Can't very well refuse under those circumstances, can I?

Alex Of course not.

Don Does that answer your question?

Alex Completely.

The Colonel enters

Colonel The taxi's here, Mr Peters. (*He sees Alex*) Oh, hello Alex. (*To Don*) Mrs McEwan's gone out to meet her. Have you finished your work?

Don No. But I'll finish it later. (*He starts to collect up his papers and put them into his briefcase*)

Colonel There's no need to rush off immediately. You ... er ... might like to stay a minute or two. Just to wish her well. I'm sure she'd appreciate it.

Don No, I don't think so. Not at the moment.

Colonel Then later perhaps?

Don Perhaps.

He goes off

Colonel Hm. Just as well. He probably wouldn't be very welcome. He's not the sort of chap you can readily take to, is he?

Alex (*who has not been listening*) I'm sorry I didn't hear ...

Colonel Mr Peters. I said he's not a very likeable character.

Alex (*softly*) No.

Colonel Mind you, I suppose we're all a bit prejudiced. Can't be expected to like someone who's turned your world upside down. It isn't human nature, is it?

Alex (*softly*) Isn't it?

Colonel But we shouldn't really judge him by that. He's got an unpleasant job to do. If it hadn't been him it'd have been someone else. There's no stopping progress these days. All the same it would have helped if the Venture ... what's it ... Company had sent someone with a more attractive personality. Someone not quite so ... er ...

Alex Indifferent?

Colonel That's not the word I was after. Dedicated. That's it. Dedicated. Dedicated to doing a job that a normal person would hate. Ah well, I suppose it takes all sorts to make a world.

Mrs O'Neil enters. She is carrying her rug which is now complete

Mrs O'Neil Well? Where is she? I though she'd be in here.

Colonel Mrs McEwan took her into her sitting-room. She'll be here presently.

Mrs O'Neil If I'd known I wouldn't have galloped upstairs when I saw the taxi. I'm still out of breath.

Colonel I don't know why you had to go rushing upstairs.

Mrs O'Neil To get the last bit of wool for me rug.

Colonel Oh, I see.

Mrs O'Neil Well we'd better not all stand round looking like a reception committee.

Colonel Even though we are one?

Mrs O'Neil Of course not. We must all be as casual and natural as possible. To put her at her ease. It'd help if we all sat down.

The Colonel goes to sit in the chair above the stove

Not in that one, Colonel!

Colonel Of course not. Sorry.

They all sit, leaving the chair above the stove empty. There is an awkward silence for a few moments

Mrs O'Neil We ought to be doing something. We can't just sit around like stuffed dummies.

Colonel (*pointing to the rug which is rolled up on Mrs O'Neil's lap*) You could be doing your rug.

Mrs O'Neil I've finished it. Upstairs. Just now.

Colonel Oh. I see.

Mrs O'Neil You could be reading your *Daily Telegraph.*

Colonel I finished it. After breakfast.

Mrs O'Neil Including the crossword?

Colonel After lunch.

Mrs O'Neil Oh. I see. (*A pause*) Now if only one of us could play the piano.

Colonel Alex?

Alex shakes her head

Mrs O'Neil Your mother ought to be here. Then you could sing. Miss Fanner loves to hear you sing. So do I. I don't suppose you could sing without accompaniment?

Alex (*shaking her head*) No.

Mrs O'Neil Pity. I've missed hearing you rehearse over the last few days. Since you gave up the idea of attending the audition. I suppose it's too late now. Even if you changed your mind.

Alex Yes, it is too late. The audition's this afternoon.

Mrs O'Neil What a shame. You've got a lovely voice, you know. I'm sure the Colonel agrees with me.

Colonel I certainly do. I've particularly enjoyed listening to the songs you've been singing recently.

Alex The Indian Love Lyrics?

Colonel That's them. Couldn't remember the name. My wife used to sing them.

Mrs O'Neil The one about the kingfisher?

Colonel And the other one. Can remember how it went but can't remember what it's called. My wife used to sing it in the Club at Hazaribagh. I can see her now. Sitting at the piano. She could play as well as sing, you know. How did it go? (*Reciting slowly*) "Pale hands I love beside the Shalimar ..." They were too. Pale, long and slender. Translucent almost in the lamplight. I can still see them in that moment of silence before the applause as the music died away and they came to rest slowly, in her lap. "Where are you now? Who lies beneath your spell?" (*He is suddenly self-conscious*) I'm sorry. Stupid of me. Silly how a few soppy sentimental words bring back the past.

Mrs O'Neil Of course it isn't. That's all we've got.

Mrs McEwan enters followed by Miss Fanner

Colonel (*rising to his feet*) Miss Fanner!

Mrs O'Neil Why, you're looking fine!

Alex Hello, Miss Fanner.

Colonel (*crossing to her and leading her to the chair above the stove*) Come and sit down. We've kept your chair for you.

Miss Fanner Thank you. (*She sits*) Thank you so much.

Mrs McEwan If it isn't warm enough for her, Colonel, give me a shout and I'll come and make the stove up.

Colonel I will.

Mrs McEwan exits

Well, now ...

There is a pause

Miss Fanner (*fiddling in her handbag*) How much do I owe you, Colonel?

Colonel Owe me? Owe me for what?

Miss Fanner The taxi. The driver wouldn't let me pay. He said he'd been paid already. I assume it was you.

Colonel It was nothing. Only a few pence. It's not worth bothering about.

Miss Fanner I insist on paying. You must tell me exactly how much.

Colonel Forget it please.

Miss Fanner But you've done so much already. All those lovely flowers ...

Colonel They weren't all from me. Only the little bunch.

Miss Fanner The orange blossom?

Colonel That's right. The carnations were from Mrs McEwan and the roses from Mrs O'Neil.

Miss Fanner (*to Mrs O'Neil*) Thank you my dear. They were lovely.

Mrs O'Neil Och, it was nothing.

Colonel And the fruit came from Mrs Roski.

Miss Fanner I must thank her. Where is she?

Colonel She'll be here soon. She had an appointment at the American Embassy just after lunch.

Miss Fanner And all the letters. There was one from you, Alex. Thank you my dear. You've all been so kind. So very very kind. I feel awful.

Mrs O'Neil Awful? What are you feeling awful about?

Miss Fanner Putting you all to so much trouble.

Mrs O'Neil Trouble? Now why should it be trouble. We enjoyed doing it. What's a few flowers and a bit of fruit, anyway? It's the least we could do. If ever I get carried off to hospital I'll expect you all to do the same. And just for the record it's roses I like. Pink but preferably red. And grapes. Big black ones. None of them little green sour beggars all full of pips.

Colonel (*with a smile*) We'll remember. But I doubt whether we'll ever see you in hospital.

Mrs O'Neil And why ever not pray?

Colonel Because you're too healthy.

Mrs O'Neil Me? Healthy? You must be joking. I'm full of the most terrible aches and pains. You should see the varicose veins on me left leg. If it wasn't for me elastic stocking I'd never be able to get about. If I showed them to a doctor I'd be inside like a shot. Anyway none of us can tell what'll happen to us from one day to the next. Look at Miss Fanner. Hale and hearty one minute. Off on a stretcher the next. You never can tell. It might be my turn this very evening. I might fall down the stairs and break my neck. Accidents happen to the best of us.

Miss Fanner But that's it. Don't you see? That's why I feel so ashamed at all the trouble I've caused. It wasn't an accident. I took those pills deliberately.

Colonel In a state of shock.

Miss Fanner What difference does that make?

Colonel It means you weren't responsible for your actions. You didn't know what you were doing at the time.

Miss Fanner Oh, but I did. I knew all right. I wanted to die.

Mrs O'Neil And therefore we shouldn't have done what we did? Eh? Is that what you're trying to say? We should have said to ourselves "Serve the silly old fool right. She's brought it on herself. She doesn't deserve flowers or fruit or letters or anything". Is that what you really think?

Miss Fanner I don't know ... I ...

Mrs O'Neil If it is then you've a pretty poor opinion of us all.

Miss Fanner (*almost in tears*) Don't ... please don't.

Mrs O'Neil Don't what?

Miss Fanner Don't be kind any more. It makes it all so much harder ...

Mrs O'Neil Harder? To what? To feel sorry for yourself? To feel lonely and unwanted? My God do you think we haven't all felt the same ourselves? Do you think we've never reached the point you've reached? And then did nothing about it because we hadn't the courage to do what you've tried to do.

Miss Fanner I don't believe that.

Mrs O'Neil Then why do you think we go on?

Miss Fanner You've a future. That's why you go on. You've something to look forward to. Something to live for.

Mrs O'Neil And you haven't?
Miss Fanner No. Not any more.

Mrs O'Neil gets up and goes to her. She thrusts her rolled-up rug into Miss Fanner's lap. The rain gradually begins to lessen

Mrs O'Neil (*sharply*) There!
Miss Fanner What is it?
Mrs O'Neil You know what it is. It's me rug.
Miss Fanner (*unrolling it*) You've finished it.
Mrs O'Neil Yes. There's a bald patch on your carpet just beside your bed. It'll cover it up nicely. Keep your feet warm when you get up in the morning. That's something to live for. Warm feet.
Miss Fanner You mean you're giving it to me?
Mrs O'Neil Course I'm giving it to you. Don't you like it?
Miss Fanner Like it? It's lovely. The best one you've done. But I couldn't accept it.
Mrs O'Neil Why not?
Miss Fanner It's for your daughter.
Mrs O'Neil No it's not. It's for you.
Miss Fanner But you said you were making it for her.
Mrs O'Neil Did I now?
Miss Fanner Like all the others.
Mrs O'Neil I've never made one for me daughter in me life. Where she is she doesn't need a rug. And even if I gave her one she wouldn't thank me for it.
Miss Fanner But we all thought ...
Mrs O'Neil That I sent them off to her ...
Miss Fanner In India.
Mrs O'Neil And that someday soon she was coming home for good. And I was going to buy a little house somewhere near her so I could settle down and enjoy me grandchildren in me old age?
Miss Fanner Yes. That's what we all believed.
Mrs O'Neil That's what I meant you to believe. Even though I didn't believe it myself. And you know why? Because I was ashamed to tell you the truth. But I'll tell it to you now. So you can see what sort of a future I've got to look forward to. I make them rugs to sell. To make a few extra quid to supplement me pension. I've never sent one to me daughter because for over fifteen years I didn't know where she was. But I know now. I've known for over a year. She's in a Belfast jail. Serving a ten-year stretch. For helping the man she lived with to put a bomb under a police sergeant's car. (*A pause*) And now I'll go and look at me lilies.

She goes off into the garden

Miss Fanner (*getting to her feet and taking a step or two after her*) Mrs O'Neil ...
Colonel No. Leave her!
Miss Fanner But I can't just ... (*She looks at the rug*)
Colonel Keep it. She wants you to have it. Put it by your bed as she suggested. She'll be hurt if you don't. And I'll be hurt too if you don't

accept this. (*Somewhat shyly he brings a small bottle of brandy out of his pocket and holds it out to her*)

Miss Fanner Oh Colonel! No really ...

Colonel Go on. Take it.

She takes it

It's nothing much. Just a small bottle. But the best. Put it on your bedside table and take a wee drop whenever you're feeling depressed. I do it. Always have done. Ever since I kept a cellar. Wouldn't be without it.

Miss Fanner A whole bottle of brandy!

Colonel Half a bottle.

Miss Fanner Really I can't ...

Colonel Why? Don't you like brandy?

Miss Fanner Yes but ... It's so long since I've had any.

Colonel That's soon remedied. Have a shot now. We'll all have a shot. Alex! Go and talk nicely to Mrs McEwan. See if you can get her to lend us some glasses.

Alex goes off

Miss Fanner (*sitting down and spreading the rug out on her knees*) She's spent every moment for the past three months working on this. And apart from the time she must have spent pounds on the wool. It's far too much to give away.

Colonel Surely that's for her to decide.

Miss Fanner She shouldn't have done it. It makes me feel awful.

Colonel Dammit woman! Stop thinking of yourself. Her rugs are her life. They're the only things she's got. Giving you one is the only way she can show what she feels about you. Particularly as you've always admired them so much.

Miss Fanner I've admired them all. Every one she's made. (*A pause*) Did you know about her daughter?

Colonel No.

Miss Fanner She'd never have told us if it hadn't been for me. Trying to show I wasn't the only one ...

Colonel Of course you're not the only one. We all have moments of despair. But we don't all take the easy way out. We go on. Time helps. But never completely. The scar remains. Even after ten years ...

Miss Fanner You mean ... your wife.

Colonel She's incurable. In a mental home.

Miss Fanner But I thought ...

Colonel Oh, I know what you thought. You thought what I told you.

Miss Fanner Her heart. That's what you said ...

Colonel True, I suppose. If hearts can be broken.

Miss Fanner I'm sorry ... I didn't know ...

Colonel You weren't meant to know. But there's no reason why you shouldn't. She blames me you see.

Miss Fanner Blames you?

Colonel For killing our only son. By kicking him out of the house in a fit of temper. Telling him never to come back. He didn't. He smashed himself up on his motor cycle. Ten minutes later. She's never forgiven me.

Miss Fanner So you'll never go home ...?

Colonel Home?

Miss Fanner To your estate in Surrey.

Colonel It doesn't exist. Never has done. We lived in a detached house in Farnham. It was sold years ago. So you see you're not alone. No-one's alone. Moments of despair come to us all. It's getting beyond despair that matters.

Miss Fanner That's easy to say. Easy for you.

Colonel Easy?

Miss Fanner Easy for you and Mrs O'Neil.

Colonel It's not easy for anyone.

Mrs Roski enters and unseen by them listens to their conversation

Miss Fanner But don't you see? Don't you see that in spite of what you've both said you've proved nothing? It's different for me.

Colonel Why?

Miss Fanner Because you've got a future. You've both got a future.

Colonel No more than you.

Miss Fanner Far more than me. Your wife's still alive. She may need you. She may even get better. Miracles do happen.

Colonel Very rarely.

Miss Fanner But as long as you've got hope you can keep going. It's enough to live for.

Colonel And Mrs O'Neil?

Miss Fanner Has her daughter.

Colonel Who doesn't care twopence for her.

Miss Fanner But someday she might. That's the whole point. There's always that hope. But for me ... what hope is there for me?

Mrs Roski You do not need hope.

Miss Fanner (*turning and seeing her for the first time*) Mrs Roski!

Mrs Roski Hope is a delusion. It is sufficient to be alive.

Miss Fanner Alive?

Mrs Roski To feel the sun on your face and the vind in your hair. To be conscious of another day.

Miss Fanner I don't believe it! And neither do you!

Mrs Roski I do. I believe it vith all my heart.

Miss Fanner How can you believe it when you've lived on hope all these years? The hope of finding your son again.

Mrs Roski And now he is found.

Colonel Found?

Mrs Roski This afternoon I 'ave seen his photograph. At the American Embassy. A fine boy. Just like his father. Tall and fair.

Miss Fanner Oh, I'm so glad for you.

Colonel We both are.

Mrs Roski I too am glad to 'ave seen him. It is something. Something to remember.

Miss Fanner Remember?

Mrs Roski I am not going to America.

Miss Fanner You mean he is coming here?

Mrs Roski No.

Miss Fanner But you must ...

Mrs Roski There is no point. 'E died six months ago. Of polio, I think you call it. Oh God ...

There is a pause

Alex enters with a tray of glasses

Alex I'm afraid they're all shapes and sizes. (*Seeing Mrs Roski*) Oh, Mrs Roski, I didn't know you were here. I didn't include you when I counted up. But don't worry. There's a few extra I think. Mainly tumblers I'm afraid. Nothing approaching a brandy glass among them.

Colonel I doubt whether Mrs Roski will be wanting to drink with us ...

Mrs Roski Vhy not? When you are celebrating?

Miss Fanner It's not exactly a celebration ...

Colonel Of course it is. We're celebrating Miss Fanner's return.

Mrs Roski Then I vill certainly drink to that. Ve 'ave missed you so much.

Miss Fanner (*in a small voice, blinking back tears*) Thank you. Everyone's so kind. It's the Colonel's idea. He bought the brandy.

Colonel And now I'm going to open it. (*He opens the bottle and starts to pour it into the glasses*)

Mrs Roski I 'ope it vill go round.

Colonel Don't worry about that. I've a reserve supply in my bedroom. (*Handing out glasses*) There you are, Mrs Roski.

Mrs Roski Thank you.

Colonel And one for you, Miss Fanner.

Miss Fanner Thank you. I can't remember when I last drank brandy ...

Colonel Neither can I ...

Miss Fanner But you just said ...

Colonel In the afternoon I mean. Alex?

Alex (*taking the glass*) Thank you.

Colonel Not that I ever drink much in the evening either. It's only there for medicinal purposes. Trouble is I never seem to be ill. All supplied? Right then ...

Miss Fanner Wait! Mrs O'Neil! We can't drink without her.

Colonel You're quite right. Of course we can't. Hang on. I'll get her.

He goes off through the french windows

Miss Fanner (*to Mrs Roski*) She's so thoughtful. She's given me this rug. For my bedroom.

Mrs Roski It vill keep your feet warm.

Miss Fanner That's just what she said. I'm quite overwhelmed. You've all been so ... so understanding. Oh! The fruit! How ungracious of me. I've forgotten to thank you.

Mrs Roski You like peaches?

Miss Fanner I love them. They're my favourite luxury.

Mrs Roski I'm glad.

Mrs O'Neil enters through the french windows, followed by the Colonel

Mrs O'Neil What's all this then? Drinking in the afternoon! I've never heard of such a thing. Whose idea is it?
Miss Fanner The Colonel's. He bought the bottle.
Colonel Half a bottle!
Miss Fanner You'll join us won't you?
Mrs O'Neil Of course I will. I never say no to a wee nip. Even in the afternoon. But I warn you. I've no head for drink. A couple of tots and me glasses steam up. Two more and I'm singing. If I go over that I'm horizontal.
Colonel No fear of that. Even with my reserves upstairs the supply won't stretch that far.
Mrs O'Neil Pity. I haven't been horizontal for years.

The Colonel hands her a glass

Thank you.
Colonel Well now, we all seem to be supplied ...
Mrs O'Neil (*raising her glass*) Cheers everyone!
Colonel No wait! This is an occasion. I think it calls for a toast.
Mrs Rosi (*raising her glass*) To Miss Fanner ...
Colonel Whom we're so glad to have back with us ...
Miss Fanner (*blinking back tears*) No ... Please ... Not to me ...
Colonel To the future then ...
Mrs Roski And those of us starting all over again ...
Mrs O'Neil The future!

They all drink except Alex

Colonel Come on Alex. Drink up. Your future's got more promise than all of ours put together.

Alex puts down her glass with a short laugh which turns into a strangled sob

Alex!
Mrs O'Neil What's the matter dear? Are you all right?
Alex (*quickly recovering herself*) Yes ... yes I'm fine ...
Mrs O'Neil If you're not feeling well ...
Alex I'm perfectly all right. I'm sorry. It was stupid of me ... Where's my glass. (*She picks up her glass and raises it*) To the future! To spring in the City, summer in the country and winter in France ... (*She drinks*)
Colonel Bravo!

Mrs Dalmahoy enters, carrying a plant in a pot which is carefully wrapped in white paper bearing the printed name of a florist's shop

Outside the rain has stopped and the sun is starting to break through the clouds. From now until the curtain, the light outside starts to increase

Ah Mrs Dalmahoy! You're just in time.
Mrs O'Neil We're having a drink.

Colonel To welcome Miss Fanner back.

Miss Fanner You'll join us I hope.

Mrs Dalmahoy Thank you . . . no.

Colonel We've got a spare glass . . .

Mrs Dalmahoy Thank you. But I don't drink. I came in to see Miss Fanner . . . I'm glad you've recovered. You . . . er . . . look fine.

Miss Fanner I am.

Mrs Dalmahoy I didn't send you anything when you were in hospital. And I'm not going to apologize. Because I did it deliberately. I know what it's like in hospital. You always get more than enough of everything. And then leave it all behind. So I decided to wait. Until you came out. To give you this. (*She holds out the wrapped plant*)

Miss Fanner (*taking it*) Thank you.

Mrs Dalmahoy Keep it that way up. And be careful when you unwrap it. It's a bit fragile.

Miss Fanner It's very kind . . .

Mrs Dalmahoy Not at all. Now please excuse me. I have some letters to write . . . (*She turns to go*)

Alex Mother!

Mrs Dalmahoy (*turning*) Yes? What is it?

Alex Can't you write them later?

Mrs Dalmahoy I want to catch the post.

Alex Then I'll have to go alone.

Mrs Dalmahoy Alone? Where?

Alex The audition.

Mrs Dalmahoy (*looking at her watch*) Don't be ridiculous. There isn't time.

Alex Yes there is. We've over an hour.

Mrs Dalmahoy But you haven't rehearsed . . .

Alex I'll get through it all right . . .

Mrs Dalmahoy You . . . you really mean it?

Alex Of course I mean it.

Mrs Dalmahoy Then don't just stand there! Get upstairs quick and change.

Alex moves to the door

The red dress. You must wear your red. With the black and silver belt. It's in the wardrobe. At the right-hand side. (*She follows Alex to the door*) Well, go on!

Alex runs off

(*Calling after her*) It's in a polythene dust jacket! (*She turns to the others*) What can you do with a girl like that? Never knows her mind from one minute to the next.

Mrs Dalmahoy goes off

The Colonel and Mrs O'Neil turn to Miss Fanner who is sitting holding her gift. She starts to unwrap it carefully. The plant is revealed. It is a small azalea in full bloom. Miss Fanner gazes at it for a moment or two, then holds it up and starts to admire it. A smile spreads slowly across her face. A shaft of sunlight comes through the window. The Colonel crosses to the window and looks out

Colonel The sun's coming out, the weatherman was right. It's going to be a fine day after all!

CURTAIN

FURNITURE AND PROPERTY LIST

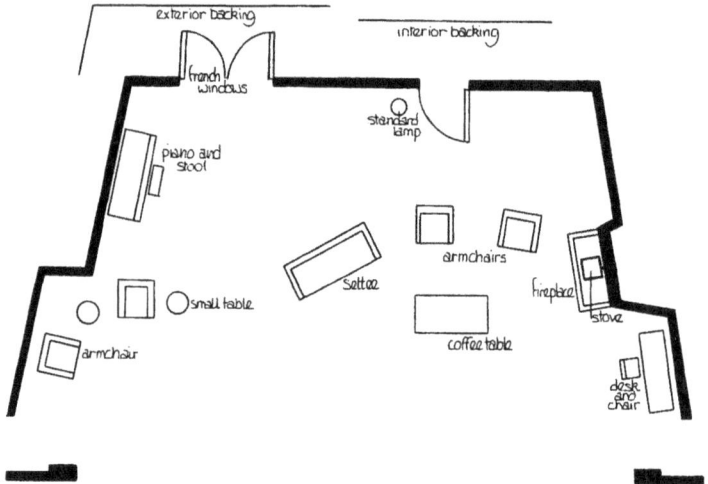

ACT I

SCENE 1

On stage: Piano. *On it:* sheet music. *On top:* pile of music and magazines
Small table. *On it:* radio
Fireplace. *In hearth:* slow combustion stove. *On mantelpiece:* ornaments
Several easy chairs. *On them:* cushions
Settee. *On it:* cushions
Writing desk. *On it:* visitors' book, pen
Upright chair
Coffee table. *On it:* ashtray
Occasional tables. *On one:* pile of books
On walls: pictures
Standard lamp
Carpet
Window curtains (*open*)

Off stage: Book **(Don)**
Uncompleted rug and wool **(Mrs O'Neil)**
Music **(Mrs Dalmahoy)**

Personal: **Mrs Dalmahoy:** wrist-watch
Don: cigarette case containing cigarettes; lighter

SCENE 2

Strike: Dirty ashtray

Set: Clean ashtray
Rug and wool for **Mrs O'Neil**
Magazine containing 2 sheets of music for **Miss Fanner**

Off stage: Letter **(Miss Fanner)**
2 letters **(Colonel)**
Letter **(Mrs Roski)**
Crushed and broken azalea **(Miss Fanner)**

Personal: **Mrs O'Neil:** wrist-watch, handbag containing letter

ACT II

SCENE 1

Strike: Azalea
All letters

Set: Documents, papers, briefcase on desk
Window curtains closed

Off stage: Tray with plate of sandwiches, glass of milk **(Mrs McEwan)**

Personal: **Don:** key

SCENE 2

Set: Window curtains open
Rug and wool for **Mrs O'Neil**
Book for **Mrs Dalmahoy**

Off stage: Briefcase with plan, pocket calculator, notebook, pencil, tape measure,
scale **(Don)**
Completed rug **(Mrs O'Neil)**
Tray of glasses **(Alex)**
Wrapped plant **(Mrs Dalmahoy)**

Personal: **Colonel:** wrist-watch, half-bottle of brandy in pocket
Don: handkerchief
Miss Fanner: handbag
Mrs Dalmahoy: wrist-watch

LIGHTING PLOT

Property fittings required: wall brackets, standard lamp

Interior. A lounge. The same scene throughout

ACT I, SCENE 1. Early evening

To open: general interior lighting

No cues

ACT I, SCENE 2. Afternoon

To open: general interior lighting

No cues

ACT II, SCENE 1. Evening

To open: general interior lighting; wall brackets and standard lamp on

No cues

ACT II, SCENE 2. Early afternoon

To open: dull, general lighting

Cue 1	**Mrs Dalmahoy** enters *Bring up sunlight effect outside french windows—gradually increase*	(Page 47)
Cue 2	**Miss Fanner** unwraps plant *Shaft of sunlight through french windows*	(Page 49)

EFFECTS PLOT

ACT I

Cue 1   **Mrs O'Neil** switches on radio   (Page 17)
          Snap on loud music

Cue 2   **Mrs O'Neil** turns up radio   (Page 17)
          Increase volume of music

Cue 3   **Mrs O'Neil** switches off radio   (Page 17)
          Snap off music

ACT II

Cue 4   As SCENE 2 opens   (Page 35)
          Rain effect outside french windows—continue until next cue

Cue 5   **Mrs O'Neil** thrusts rug into **Miss Fanner**'s lap   (Page 43)
          Begin gradual fade of rain effect

www.ingramcontent.com/pod-product-compliance
Lightning Source LLC
LaVergne TN
LVHW051806080426
835511LV00019B/3420